MW01039531

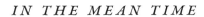

IN THE MEAN TIME

Postwestern Horizons

IN the
MEAN
TIME

Temporal Colonization
and the Mexican American
Literary Tradition

ERIN MURRAH-MANDRIL

University of Nebraska Press · Lincoln

An earlier version of chapter 1 was published as "Ruiz
de Burton's 'Contemporary Novel': Multifarious
Time in *The Squatter and the Don*," *Aztlán: A
Journal of Chicano Studies* 41, no. 2 (2016): 37–
63. © Regents of the University of California.
Published by the UCLA Chicano Studies Research
Center Press. Reprinted with permission.

Library of Congress Cataloging-in-Publication Data
Names: Murrah-Mandril, Erin, author.
Title: In the mean time: temporal colonization
and the Mexican American literary
tradition / Erin Murrah-Mandril.
Description: Lincoln: University of Nebraska
Press, [2020] | Series: Postwestern horizons |
Includes bibliographical references and index.
Identifiers: LCCN 2019032954 | ISBN 9781496211828
(hardback) | ISBN 9781496221711 (epub) | ISBN
9781496221728 (mobi) | ISBN 9781496221735 (pdf)
Subjects: LCSH: American literature—20th
century—History and criticism. | American
literature—Mexican American authors—History
and criticism. | Space and time in literature. |
Mexican-American Border Region—In literature. |
| Mexican Americans—Intellectual life.
Classification: LCC PS153.M4 M87
2020 | DDC 810.9/005—dc23
LC record available at https://lccn.loc.gov/2019032954

Set in Garamond Premier by Mikala R. Kolander.
Designed by N. Putens.

For Chris
For all time

CONTENTS

PREFACE

The experience of writing *In the Mean Time* has been as recursive as the historical texts I explore in the book, and in many ways writing it has prompted a personal rendition of literary-historical recovery. In the spring of 2017, well into the production of *In the Mean Time*, I found a 1986 article by Hector A. Torres titled "Discourse and Plot in Rolando Hinojosa's *The Valley*: Narrativity and the Recovery of Chicano Heritage." Torres argues that *The Valley* has a configurational plot rather than an episodic plot. The configurational plot, Torres explains, is purposeful and whole, not anarrative, as some might assume, and it constitutes a retrieval of the "most fundamental potentialities" of our past (87). The terminology and theory were different, but the underlying idea was strikingly similar to what I had been working on for the past few years. Hector Torres had been one of my graduate mentors, but he was murdered in March 2010. He introduced me to literary theory over the course of three graduate classes and many unofficial discussions over a pint of beer. I never studied Chicana/o literature with him; I had taken his courses on literary theory, grammar, and narratology. When I found Dr. Torres's article, it presented the all-too-common but very uncanny experience of seeing my own thought process constituted in a past that I never knew about, like a lost intellectual inheritance. It was a moment of recovery and the kind of recursive repetition Dr. Torres often theorized.

If I am completely honest, the focus in chapter 3 on specters emerged from a desire to channel Dr. Torre's intellectual spirit, his impressive and perplexing grasp of Derridian philosophy, while also reckoning with his untimely death.

More broadly, *In the Mean Time* tackles the question of how to continue learning from someone who is no longer alive. My belated encounter with Hector Torres's article was not the only instance of coming across scholarly work late into the project that I should probably have read early on and of feeling like I was merely retracing the steps of my intellectual forbearers. Scholars often experience this process but usually hide it to make our hermeneutic circle appear more complete, our writing more seamless. I hope it is hidden in my work as well, but I also hope the imprint and the influence of my mentors are writ large across the pages of *In the Mean Time*.

In that vein I would first like to thank Jesse Alemán, whose intellectual generosity and savvy advice are beyond measure. I couldn't imagine a more perfect mentor. I am also grateful for the support and guidance of José Aranda. Likewise, the faculty, staff, and students at the UT Arlington Center for Mexican American Studies have made me feel at home in Texas (no easy task for a New Mexican), and the center has provided financial support for archival research. I especially want to thank Christian Zlolniski, Ignacio Ruiz-Pérez, Cristina Salinas, and Isabel Montemayor for their feedback on multiple chapters and professional guidance. David LaFevor, Ana Gregorio Cano, Marcela Nava, and Alicia Rueda-Acedo also provided helpful advice for parts of the manuscript. The Posthumanism Research Cluster in the UTA English Department workshopped chapter 2. Thank you to Jackie Fey, Stacy Alaimo, Neill Matheson, and Jason Hogue. I would also like to thank Belinda Rincón for her detailed review of the manuscript and support of the project. Thank you to the anonymous readers whose incisive critiques helped me clarify and hone the book's thesis.

The editorial staff at the University of Nebraska Press has been wonderful. I would especially like to thank Alicia Christensen for shepherding the project from proposal to print. The Center for Regional Studies Hector Torres Fellowship provided financial support for this project early on. The Feminist Research Institute at the University of New Mexico also helped fund archival research in the early stages of this project. I am grateful to Recovering the U.S. Hispanic Literary Heritage and all the scholars who publish and promote early Latina/o literature. The biennial Recovery Conference has been an invaluable space for thinking through the ideas in this book.

I am thankful to have a community of academic women who share their knowledge with me regularly. Leigh Johnson, my dear friend, mentor, and sometimes doppelganger, has read more drafts than I can count and taught me about motherwork—how to value my own and appreciate others'. Melina Vizcaíno-Alemán and Karen Roybal helped me articulate my thoughts into the form of a book. Marissa López taught me the value of a through line. Lorena Gauthereau has sharpened my research skills. Noreen Diana Rivera, Bernadine Hernandez, Myrriah Gomez, Lindsey Ives, Robin Runia, and Amanda Ellis have each provided support and shaped the ideas of this work at various points.

My family has shown me that "in the meantime," life and love go on. I am thankful to my mother, who gave me the foundation to pursue a life that women in my family had previously only dreamed of. Sam, you arrived in the world just as this project was beginning and revolutionized my understanding of time. Noah, your joy is magical. Abby, tomorrow is here; thank you for your patience. To Christopher, there are not enough words to express my gratitude.

Introduction

The Mean Time of U.S. Modernity

The record for the longest continuous filibuster in the U.S. Senate is held by Strom Thurmond, who spoke for twenty-four hours and eighteen minutes to impede the Civil Rights Act of 1957. But in 1903 a U.S. filibuster against New Mexico statehood lasted for three months. Miguel Antonio Otero, governor of the Hispano-majority U.S. territory, watched as his home's chance for political enfranchisement slipped away.[1] The bill under review would have granted New Mexicans the right to vote in federal elections and select their own governor and congressional representatives. Review of the bill had begun in June of the previous year, when Governor Otero listened to the senators describe New Mexico's iconic adobe architecture by discussing "the Mexican population . . . living in mud houses, just as they did one hundred years ago."[2] The Senate sustained the monumental filibuster by manipulating its schedule. Senators agreed to divide the day into two sections. General legislation proceeded each morning until two o'clock, after which the Senate commenced reviewing or, rather, delaying the statehood bill as time ticked away in the congressional session. While depicting New Mexico as backward and premodern, members of the Committee on Territories installed the very economic and political underdevelopment they described with their own tactics of purposeful delay. It is no coincidence that both Strom Thurmond and the Senate Committee on Territories used their ability to control time toward the racist ends of denying full citizen rights to people of color.

Historically, the United States has used time as a weapon of colonization to exclude people of color from participation in the nation's past, present, and future. National historical amnesia writes people of color out of history books and the popular imagination of national development; political manipulations of time, like the New Mexico filibuster, bar people of color from participating in political and economic processes in the present; and together, combined with state violence, these tactics attempt to erase people of color from the national future. *In the Mean Time* explores the U.S. processes of colonizing Mexican Americans' time in the late nineteenth and early twentieth centuries. The process was both material and ideological, restructuring Mexican Americans' lived experiences through new schedules, new procedures, and new narratives of social belonging. These changes contributed significantly to the racialization of Mexican Americans that occurred during this period.

In the Mean Time draws its title from the 1848 Treaty of Guadalupe Hidalgo that concluded the U.S.-Mexico War and ceded over five hundred thousand square miles of Mexican territory to the United States. That land was inhabited by nearly one hundred thousand Mexican citizens, most of whom remained in their homes as the U.S.-Mexico border moved southward, across them. When Congress ratified the Treaty of Guadalupe Hidalgo, it infamously removed article 10, which had been designed to protect the land rights of former Mexican citizens. It also revised language in article 9 concerning Mexican Americans' U.S. citizenship. Article 9 originally stated that Mexicans who remained in the new U.S. territories would be "admitted *as soon as possible* . . . to the enjoyment of all the rights of the U.S. citizens of the United States" (italics added), but the Senate removed "as soon as possible" and replaced it with "at the proper time (to be judged by the Congress of the United States)." Both versions of article 9 stated that "in the mean time" former Mexicans would be "maintained and protected in the free enjoyment of their liberty and their property" (Griswold del Castillo 1990, 179–81). This seemingly minor revision deferred full citizenship rights for Mexican Americans to an unspecified "proper time," held hostage by congressional and judiciary systems more focused on delaying and removing Mexican Americans' rights. The United States' failure to grant Mexican Americans equal citizenship rights extended the treaty's "mean time" indefinitely. *In the Mean Time* excavates the post-treaty period as a locus of temporal manipulation that excluded Mexican Americans from U.S. modernity by exploring the narrative time of a Californiana, a Nuevomexicano, and two Tejana writers living in this period who worked to reinsert Mexican Americans into national historical narratives. More important, their writing demonstrates that chronology, progress, causality, and other forms of time are constructions to be remade for the purpose of survival and self-representation.

The deferral of full political enfranchisement for Mexican Americans to the "proper time" was especially significant for Nuevomexicanos, whose territory was denied statehood for more than fifty years despite numerous appeals to Congress. But Mexican Americans residing in states such as California and Texas, which were admitted to the Union quickly, also rarely experienced equal rights, despite their legal designation. It would seem that the "proper time" never actually arrived for Mexican Americans, who "in the mean time" were positioned outside U.S. modernity and its narratives of historical development, industrial progress, and political process. In this way the mean time became a kind of temporal limbo during which Mexican Americans were systematically disenfranchised by laws, such as the 1851 California Land Act, which forced Californios to legitimate their land holdings in lengthy U.S. court battles, draining Californio ranchers of their financial resources and forcing them to mortgage their land away even if their grants were ultimately confirmed. Mexican Americans' liberty was also eroded through California's Anti-Vagrancy Act, also known as the "Greaser Act," which effectively made it illegal for lower-class Mexican Americans to congregate or have leisure time outside of their homes; the New Mexico statehood filibuster described earlier that stalled financial investment in the territory and enabled political corruption; de facto segregation in Southwest public schools; and lynching, especially by the Texas Rangers, whose "brutal repression of the Mexican population was tantamount to state-sanctioned terrorism" (Carrigan and Webb 2003, 417).

In the mean time Anglo artists and politicians alike depicted Mexican Americans as a people of the past, slow and incapable of participating in modern economic and political processes. In this way the mean time is more than a historical period; it is a mode of colonial domination—both the process of disenfranchisement and the rhetoric used to justify that process. The mean time depended on a political system that could selectively move slowly, quickly, or retroactively to usurp Mexican Americans' land and silence their political voice while at the same time criticizing Mexican Americans themselves for being economically and politically underdeveloped.

Just as the U.S.-Mexico borderlands have come to signify a site of spatial dislocation, the mean time is a site of temporal dislocation. U.S. colonization fractured the temporal structure of the U.S. Southwest by disrupting and disavowing the ways that Mexican Americans had experienced time. For example, in 1855 Francisco P. Ramírez, editor of the Los Angeles newspaper *El Clamor Público*, wrote:

Aquí en California, hemos sido favorecidos por nuestra "Legislatura Modelo," con dos leyes tan originales que no tienen igual en los fastos de ninguna nación civilizada.—Estas son la ley domingo y la famosa ley de los vagos. La primera prohíbe con pena encarcelación y multa a todos los que contravengan a sus disposiciones los bailes y otras diversiones inocentes en día domingo como para forzar al pueblo a quedarse en casa, ayunar y orar al Altísimo por nuestro bienestar. (¿no fuera mejor orar para que nos libere de tales Legislaturas?) Es verdaderamente muy ridícula la suposición que el pueblo se hace más moral quitandole sus pasatiempos o sus diversiones. [We here in California have been favored by our "Model Legislature," with two laws so original that they have no equal in the annals of any civilized nation. These are the Sunday law and the famous vagrant law. The former prohibits dances and other innocent diversions on Sunday on pain of incarceration and fine for all those who infringe on the decree, as if to force people to stay home and fast and pray to the Almighty for our welfare. (Wouldn't it be better to pray that He would free us from such legislature?) The supposition that people are made more moral by taking away their past-times and diversions is truly ridiculous.] (23)

The puritanical Sunday law regulated Mexican American time economically, as something to be *spent* according to Protestant moral values. It controlled

Mexican American bodies by regulating their time, specifically on Sunday. Ramírez's critique also hinges on the reversal of two forms of U.S. time. First, he counters, it is more righteous to pray for freedom than to restrict people's *pasatiempos*, arguing against the systemic link between morality and strictly regulated time, and, second, he implies that the United States' prized originality is actually a folly that excludes it from the "annals of any civilized nations." The Sunday law was another example of U.S. legislators using time as a weapon of colonization, and Ramírez's argument against it is fundamentally about the way that time should be organized and imagined.

Modernity and Its Forms of Time

The year 1848 was not the first instance in which time was reorganized through colonization in the borderlands of Alta California, Nuevo México, and Tejas. The region is a palimpsest of colonization, with histories of diverse indigenous peoples, Spanish colonizers, Mexican nationalists, and U.S. immigrants. Before U.S. colonization Mexico, including its northern territories, was already a modern space with its own colonial history and its own unique iterations of progress and continuity. Raúl Coronado (2013) traces a modernity rooted in Catholic Scholasticism that unfolded as historical trauma and philosophical disenchantment in eighteenth- and nineteenth-century Tejas and across the Spanish-speaking world.[3] U.S. colonization brought still other iterations of modernity rooted in providentialism and expressed through discourses of exceptionalism. The U.S. Southwest is thus a space where two forms of modernity collided, and that collision dislocated modernity as a stable source of meaning for Mexican Americans in the region.[4]

My understanding of modernity is influenced by Walter Mignolo's assertion that modernity and coloniality are two sides of the same coin, that they produce and depend on each other. Mignolo looks closely at the way modernity structured space when European colonists "invented" the Western Hemisphere through a new conception of global topography that was abstract and measurable (2005, 2). But modernity is also a way of conceptualizing time. Peter Osborne describes modernity as a "category of historical periodization . . . the first and only age that understood itself as an epoch and, in so doing, simultaneously created the other epochs" (1996, 9, 11). Modernity comes into being as a radical break from the past but also persists *as* that break in a constantly self-negating epoch of the present. Modernity's underlying temporality is empty (abstract), homogenous (measurable), and linear (progressive). But just as situated, local processes of colonization produce distinct spatial formations, they also produce diverse iterations of time. Modernity's empty, homogenous time mirrors the emptiness of Cartesian space, both of which become filled with Euro-American values as a process of colonization and modernization. Thus, while modernity is a global phenomenon (in part, a phenomenon of globalization), each situated colonial system produces a unique iteration of modernity.

It is important to read time as a situated construction, not a natural, neutral, or universal medium through which all people move in the same way, because colonialism works by normalizing its practices as universal and innate. As in Mignolo's (2005) analysis of modern space, modern time can be mapped, manipulated, and dominated. I use the terms "modernity" and "temporality" to refer to the broad system of time produced globally by the matrix of coloniality born of sixteenth-century European colonization, developed philosophically within a European scientific revolution, and promulgated through capitalist systems of exchange.[5] Modern temporality is like a grammar of time, an underlying structure that links and organizes multiple iterations of colonial time. Site-specific, socially situated iterations of time, in contrast, are like discourses, and I refer to them as "forms of time." Discursive forms of time are inflected by the specific places, people, and histories involved in their construction. Colonial forms of time may contradict one another, but they all maintain their ideological power through recourse to modernity's supposedly universal temporality of homogenous, empty, linear time. For example, U.S. railroad companies' creation of time zones depended on modernity's empty, homogenous time to arbitrarily map time onto space. Likewise, specific narratives of development—psychological, sociological, and biological—depend on modern time's linearity to prescribe a normative path of progression that authorizes certain peoples, individuals, and places as more (or less) advanced than others.

Benedict Anderson, in *Imagined Communities* (2006), describes the way the novel, the newspaper, and the nation are all dependent on modernity's empty, homogenous temporality, where disparate events and individuals coincide within a shared, uniform conception of time, explaining, "The idea of a sociological organism moving calendrically through homogenous, empty time is a precise analogue of the idea of the nation" (26). He calls this a "complex gloss upon the word 'meanwhile'" (25). But national imagined communities are more complex and uneven than this description implies. If the time of the nation is like the time of the novel, then it is a Jamesean "baggy monster" that cannibalizes residual and diverse concepts of time. Unlike the innocent "meanwhile" of coincidence, the "mean time" highlights the way that time is actively produced; it holds meaning, or intention, and in the context of colonization that intention can also be mean, as in cruel. National time comes about not primarily through the shared empty, homogenous time that citizens inhabit but through shared and co-created narratives of national belonging, which draw heavily on modernity's linear unfolding, perhaps more so than on its homogeneity. Homogeneity, in contrast, is fundamental to another component of modernity: capitalism. Homogenous, empty time lays the groundwork for capitalist abstraction, where time becomes a tool to measure and regulate labor and to calculate investment. Modernity's homogeneity helps transform time into money. Nationalism and capitalism are interrelated aspects of modernity that find expression in yet more situated and specific forms of time.

My use of the phrase "forms of time" invokes Mikhail Bakhtin's concept of the "chronotope," a narrative condensation of time and space in his theory of the novel. For Bakhtin "the primary category of the chronotope is time," and forms of time are "inherently generic"; they structure our understanding of how a narrative unfolds and how things within the narrative make meaning in relation to one another (1981, 85). Social iterations of time come together much the same way that chronotopes coalesce in novelistic dialogue. Forms of time are as diverse and multifaceted as the peoples who shape them, and in fact, a single individual usually exists within multiple social constructions of time. The specific forms of time that *In the Mean Time* examines correspond to Mexican American narratives of political and social belonging in the face of U.S. colonization. Lived experiences of time in the late nineteenth- and early twentieth-century United States were transformed by technological industrialization and social reform that shifted people's relation to family, work, religion, and nature, which all happened just as one Euro-American modernity imposed itself on another. The rapidly shifting forms of time of the late nineteenth- and early twentieth-century Southwest prompted a meta-analysis among elite Mexican American writers, who, from their vantage point of both colonizer and colonized, began to recognize and express divergent forms of time. Mexican American writing mines the disjunctures that occurred in Anglo-American attempts to control time and exposes the temporal mechanisms of U.S. colonization.

The United States had also been reorganizing divergent forms of time in the early nineteenth century. Both Lloyd Pratt's *Archives of American Time* (2010) and Thomas Allen's *A Republic in Time* (2008) look to the early nineteenth century as a period of temporal complexity, reexamining the nation's past not as a unified antecedent that would develop toward the republic's eventual territorial growth and ascendency but, instead, as a messy and sometimes conflicting network of residual and emergent uses of time that coexisted in the United States' early national imaginary. Thus, like Coronado, they aim to "question the inevitability of national formation" (2013, 18). In the latter half of the nineteenth century, though, divergent forms of time coalesced into a constellation of discursive tools that would present the United States as the bearer of modernity. This constellation is what I am calling "U.S. modernity." Allen reminds readers that John O'Sullivan, the man famous for coining the term "Manifest Destiny" in an editorial for his populist magazine, the *United States Democratic Review*, also published "The Great Nation of Futurity." Unlike O'Sullivan's other treatises on territorial expansion, in the *Democratic Review* "The Great Nation of Futurity" shores up the fact that U.S. imperialism is a project of time as much, or more than, territorial expansion. He writes, "The expansive future is our arena, and for our history. We are entering on its untrodden space with the Truths of God in our mind . . . and with a clear conscience unsullied by the past. . . . The far-reaching, the boundless future will be the era of American greatness" (1839, 428). O'Sullivan reveals the slipperiness of U.S. temporal imagining as he tries to develop a unified national narrative in the mid-nineteenth century, and his national ethos would become dominant by the twentieth century as U.S. colonization exceeded the bounds of space and attempted to colonize the future itself.

O'Sullivan (1839) describes an "untrodden" future, much like the imagined virgin wilderness of the U.S. frontier, and his depiction of an equally empty past allows the United States to chart its own history as a smooth processual narrative of progress. In reality, U.S. history, like the imagined "empty space" of the frontier, was transformed through violent processes of genocide and the forced removal of Native peoples. Building on its colonized past, the United States also colonized the present through increasingly uniform systems of timekeeping to facilitate its capitalist production and exchange. In the 1880s U.S. railroads instituted the nation's time zones. By 1918 the Standard Time Act codified these time zones and created daylight savings time.[6] This revolution in timekeeping effectively homogenized U.S. time, making it a mechanized tool of science, capitalism, and progress. These changes coincided with the systemization and institutionalization of Mexican American disenfranchisement in the U.S. Southwest. The United States mapped time, not only onto the territorialized space of time zones but also onto the people who inhabited that space. Nineteenth-century racialist discourse situated different groups of people in different forms of time. Osborne explains that "in the context of colonial experience," cultures that exist at the same historical moment "are ordered diachronically to produce a scale of development which defines 'progress' in terms of the projection of certain people's presents as other people's futures, at the level of [historical development] as a whole" (1996, 16–17). Frederick Jackson Turner codified the U.S. diachronic scale of development in his 1893 Frontier Thesis, when he claimed that "the United States lies like a huge page in the history of society. Line by line, as we read this continental page from West to East we find the record of social evolution" (1993, 66). Turner's argument that U.S. democracy stems from frontiersmen's progressive conquest of "Indians" and wilderness ignores Mexican Americans and the U.S.-Mexico War altogether, but his spatialization of progressive time projects far-western territories acquired during the war as the United States' least socially evolved region.

Differential Time Consciousness in the Borderlands

As Turner's thesis reminds us, time and space are inextricably linked concepts. To speak of one necessarily invokes the other. Mary Pat Brady describes the way that national boundaries, and specifically the U.S.-Mexico border, enforce and contain racialized time:

> National borders utilize the fantasy that a nation on one side of the border exists in one phase of temporal development while the nation on the other side functions at a different stage. Moreover, borders simultaneously produce and elide this difference between nations, implicitly suggesting that a person can be formed in one temporality but when he or she crosses a border that person transmogrifies, as it were, into someone either more or less advanced, more or less modern, more or less sophisticated.... The border exceeds understanding as a mapped geographic terrain. (2002, 50–51)

Brady's discussion of temporality along the U.S.-Mexico border describes the U.S. projection of Mexicans into a less advanced, alien temporality that renders them "ontologically impossible, outside the real and the human" (2002, 50). Yet the Treaty of Guadalupe Hidalgo moved the border—the "mapped geographic terrain" of the United States—across tens of thousands of Mexican citizens. The border at that moment fits neither Turner's 1893 progressively moving frontier, nor Brady's 2002 discussion of temporality across the long-codified U.S.-Mexico border. The nineteenth-century United States was full of so-called ontologically impossible people, not outside but within its national borders—Mexican Americans, Native peoples, African Americans, and Asian Americans were all in various ways excluded from participation in the ideological progress of U.S. modernity. Mignolo argues that the "colonization of being is nothing else than producing the idea that certain people do not belong to history—that they are non-beings" (2005, 4). An Anglo-American racial imaginary placed people of color in the sociological, if not the literal, past by excluding them from participation in national political processes and narratives of national belonging to deny people of color ontological presence within the republic. In each case U.S. colonization multiplied and fragmented temporal experience.

Though racialist rhetorics of the nineteenth century worked to exclude all people of color from modernity, racialized groups have had different relationships with U.S. modernity, depending on their unique historical experiences of colonization. Mark Rifkin (2017) examines the way settler-colonial time denies indigenous temporal sovereignty for Native Americans because both exclusion and inclusion in modern temporality inadequately address the temporal orientations of Native peoples. U.S. settler colonialism privileges modernity as either the *only* temporality or the primary temporal frame of reference against which Native peoples must define themselves. Rifkin describes, instead, multiple temporalities that each constitute their own frame of reference, and he argues for Native "temporal sovereignty" rather than temporal recognition within modernity. In contrast, Daylanne K. English argues that African American writers exist fully within U.S. modernity *and* concurrently "within a distinct temporality," in which "time and justice work together as political fiction" (2013, 3). She explains that experiences of time were unique for slaves because masters did not just regulate time but actually "owned time itself" (1). Rather than sovereignty, English looks to the importance of justice in African American writing. Both Rifkin and English describe the way that modernity is a tool of domination and an ill-fitting exclusionary temporality for people of color.

Mexican Americans' situated experience of U.S. modernity is shaped by their own complex racialization. Latinas/os, as Marissa López aptly puts it, "are legally white but socially brown" (2019, 107). Indeed, that slippage, from white to brown, is a fundamental feature of Mexican American's experiences of U.S. modernity, because it signals two competing forms of coloniality—a Mexican Spanish class-based caste system intertwined with, but not identical to, racial distinctions between Spanish and indigenous heritage and the U.S. system of rigid, pseudoscientific racial classification. Mexican American whiteness eroded during the nineteenth century, as the economic disenfranchisement of landowners (or former landowners) undermined their status-based claims to whiteness. Mexican American elites maintained a dual position and held (residual) access to the power of temporal colonization as haciendados (who had regulated forms of time on their ranchos), yet they experienced temporal colonization by the United States. José Aranda Jr. terms Mexican American's experience a "modernity of subtraction" that situates them through "loss, erosion, and dislocation" by making "*el tiempo anterior*," the time before the U.S.-Mexico War, an "irretrievable past," not only in its fullness and presence as a rich and complex sociocultural space but also in its "already evolving" future possibilities (2016, 159–60). Like the "world not to come" in Coronado's (2013) textual history of Tejas, Aranda's modernity of subtraction describes temporal dislocation.

It is within this context that I explore the writing produced by four elite Mexican Americans between 1880 and 1945. María Amparo Ruiz de Burton, Miguel Antonio Otero, Adina De Zavala, and Jovita González each had access to multiple discourses of power during a period of temporal transformation within the United States, and they each chose to engage with U.S. rhetorical constructions of history, economy, and politics that disenfranchised Mexican Americans in the "mean time" of the post-treaty Southwest. Their texts highlight the ruptures and conflicts among U.S. modernity's different forms of time. Chela Sandoval (2000) argues that colonized people are able to read signs of power to survive and contest domination. The elite Mexican American authors I discuss do not adhere to all the "technologies of oppressed" (81–82) that Sandoval describes (for example, most of them are definitely not self-consciously working toward "egalitarian democratics" [114]), but they do read and sometimes deconstruct the forms of time that support hegemonic U.S. systems of power. Sandoval calls the ability to shift between divergent ideologies "differential consciousness" (44). Early Mexican American literature performs a differential *time* consciousness that reads and deploys multiple conflicting, ideologically imbued forms of time to survive and contest U.S. domination. They do so by dialogically juxtaposing conflicting aspects of U.S. modernity.

Late nineteenth- and early twentieth-century Mexican American writing engages U.S. modernity's temporal homogenization by revealing the disjointed, conflicting forms of time that undergird national attempts to form a hegemonic narrative of progressive historical development. Their narratives are neither fluid nor linear. They disclose and often deconstruct the interconnection of progress and colonization. Their forms of time expose the United States' construction of westward expansion, national triumph, social evolution, technologic innovation, and exceptionalism as facades for domination and injustice. Yet it is also erroneous to assume that Mexican Americans were only ever outsiders to U.S. temporal formations—that they were atemporal or that there was a single form of time indicative of Mexican American temporal experience, a "Chicana/o time" of resistance or becoming. Placing Mexican American experience outside U.S. forms of time is itself a colonial practice. Indeed, U.S. colonizers are the ones who positioned Californios, Tejanos, and Nuevomexicanos outside of national time, frequently depicting Mexican Americans as lacking history, slow moving, perpetually late, and incapable of sociological development. In contrast, the Mexican American texts I encounter in this book navigate multiple and often contradictory forms of time in the Southwest to highlight the ideological underpinnings of U.S. colonization and to coordinate Mexican Americans within dominant discourses of time.

These authors' privileged social position troubled later recovery of their work in the Chicana/o literary canon. In 1998 Aranda argued that recent recovery of elite Mexican American authors "questioned anew the idea that Mexican Americans have always been proletarian in character" (553). Thus, elite Californio, Tejano, and Nuevomexicano writing disrupts linear narratives of development all the way from the nineteenth century to the twenty-first. Kirsten Silva Gruesz playfully asks, "What Was Latino Literature?" in her 2012 *PMLA* review of the *Norton Anthology of Latino Literature*, arguing that the field does not yet have a literary history. Gruesz posits that the lack of periodization within the Latino literary canon may be a sign of academic trends, where master narratives of literary history have become outmoded, or it may be that the field is still in its early development and thus working out the "temporal aspects of its ethnoracial identity" (336). I argue instead that Mexican American literature's resistance to linear narrative precedes the postmodern theoretical turn and the development of a Latina/o literary canon by more than one hundred years, as Mexican American authors of the nineteenth century navigate temporal dislocation in the wake of the Treaty of Guadalupe Hidalgo.

In the Mean Time builds on Chicana/o studies' examination of space, especially in its iteration as borderlands studies, which argues that something seemingly fixed and natural—space—is, in fact, a socially constructed medium imbued with ideological power. Time, too, is a social and ideological formation. From the syntagmatic use of verb tense to the plot of a novel, language and time are deeply interrelated. Borderlands studies corresponded with the rise of hemispheric studies and the transnational turn in American studies, all of which examine the social construction of space and the movement of people and texts throughout the Americas and around the globe. Spatial analysis is critical for examining the history of a colonized people who have been denied presence within narratives of U.S. modernity and been subject to physical dispossession and displacement within and across borders. Yet any examination of Mexican American experience or identity is incomplete without a consideration of temporality.

Genaro Padilla (1993), Leonard Pitt (1966), and Alicia Gaspar de Alba (1998) have each alluded to Mexican American temporal dislocation by describing Chicana/o or Mexican American cultural production as schizo-phrenic.[7] Padilla (1993) writes that early Mexican American narratives display an "articulatory schizophrenia" that reflects their divided subjectivity. Fredric Jameson has argued that schizophrenia is a breakdown in temporal cohesion, an aesthetic trait he ascribes to postmodernism (1991, 26–27). Yet Sandoval aptly describes Jameson's critique of postmodernity as a eulogy for the lost modernist "centered and legitimated bourgeois citizen-subject," adding that in postmodernity "the first world subject enters the kind of psychic terrain formerly inhabited by the historically decentered citizen-subject: the colonized, the outsider, the queer, the subaltern, the marginalized" (2000, 26). The his-torically decentered, dislocated time experienced by colonized subjects does not create a lack of temporal awareness or an inability to imagine diachronic relations and "organize [their] past and future into coherent experiences" the way that Jameson describes schizophrenic postmodern subjects (1991, 218) and the way that Padilla and others have described Mexican American writers.

Instead, Mexican American authors create alternative temporal imaginaries that do not depend solely on chronology for meaning. Sandoval argues that the experiences of colonized subjects give them a consciousness that can move "across and through cultural spaces" to "[migrate] between contending ideological systems" (2000, 30). While her statement focuses on spatiality as a response to Jameson's (1991) call for cognitive mapping, the same can be said of Mexican Americans' ability to move across forms of time. In fact, Sandoval's differential consciousness does have a temporal dimension that rejects linear, dialectical progression from "equal rights" to "revolutionary" to "supremacist" and "separatist" paradigms as a narrative of oppositional politics' historical development. Sandoval's differential consciousness instead draws from multiple oppositional tactics at any time and in no particular order. Likewise, early Mexican American authors move through and across different ideological formations of time, often eschewing chronology or the linear time of dialectical resolution. Their temporal adroitness should not be read in the negative connotation of schizophrenia, nor should it be displaced by an overemphasis on space. Instead, differential time consciousness is a constitutive feature of Mexican American writing, a purposeful tactic for navigating U.S. power structures.

Recovering Resistance, Resisting Recovery

The historical erasure of Mexican America's past weighs heavily on the primary texts of *In the Mean Time*. None of them were part of the U.S. American literary canon before the twenty-first century. Most of them still aren't. Mexican American literature was, in a sense, a latecomer to the recovery movements of the latter third of the twentieth century. While a number of scholars began individual work in the 1980s to find and disseminate Mexican American writing from before the Chicano Movement, their work did not effect major changes within the canon of Chicana/o literature or the broader field of American literature until the mid-1990s.[8] The recovery movement that includes Mexican American, Cuban American, Puerto Rican, and other Latina/o literatures became solidified and highly organized in the early 1990s by the Recovering the U.S. Hispanic Literary Heritage project. The project was founded as a segment of Arte Público, under director Nicolás Kanellos, and it brought together a large number of scholars invested in recovering the literary history of Latina/o authors writing in what is now the United States. Mexican American literary recovery came to fruition at an important time within the field of Chicana/o studies, a time shortly after the literary canon of the Chicano Movement had been scrutinized and transformed by a number of new influences, including the emergence of a new group of trained literary scholars, new technological innovations, large-scale investments in creating and preserving Chicana/o cultural production, and the theoretical critique of Chicana feminism.

The context of recovery is significant not only because it shapes the contemporary reception of a text but also because when the texts themselves engage with the threat of historical erasure they anticipate or enact archival recovery, articulating a metacritical dialogue with their future recovery process. Many early Mexican American texts call out to a future readership that will someday recognize their underappreciated value. For example, Otero writes in his autobiography that he "owed it to the coming generations to allow them to read first hand [his] early experiences" (1935, 287). González's and De Zavala's (1996) writings also worked to preserve Spanish and Mexican American culture for a future readership. These texts are artifacts of literary recovery both materially and thematically. Their complex forms of time exist at the nexus of composition *and* recovery.

Latina/o literary history's unease with chronology and periodization was built into the inception of the recovery project. In the inaugural edition of Arte Público's collection of critical essays (now going on ten volumes), Charles Tatum "question[ed] the usefulness of relying on, even on a temporary basis, fixed dates and the periods they encompass" (1993, 206). In 2003 Manuel Martín-Rodríguez argued that chronology and periodization in Mexican American literary history "has resulted in a sort of methodological inertia that has outlived its usefulness and that, in turn, demands the experimentation with newer approaches" (142). Scholars' aversion to master narratives of development has produced "a body of literature that doesn't yet have a literary history," as Gruesz asserts in the *Norton Anthology* review mentioned earlier. She writes, "To some degree this is a chicken-and-egg question: periodicity and canonicity have in most cases evolved alongside each other. But in the case of Latino literature, all we have is the egg" (2012, 336). But the problem of creating meaning through chronology in Chicana/o literary history is a function of the very works that make up the current canon of early Mexican American literature. These texts are difficult to periodize because they exist at the intersection of so many forms of time. Their multifarious forms of time are something to be embraced, not overcome. Thus, *In the Mean Time* is not an attempt to trace Chicana/o problems with time through history as a successive or causal relationship—indeed that would only (re)produce an equally problematic linear narrative. Instead, I wish to demonstrate that the future and the past are not so clearly delineated and that it is actually fallacious to untangle past and future to create a smooth narrative of development, particularly within a field that has had to (re)construct the past through the process of recovery.

In the Mean Time examines the entanglement of past, present, and future in Mexican American literature by focusing on narrative form. More specifically, it focuses on the dialogic interplay among multiple forms of time within each of the texts it explores. Forms of time are suffused with ideology and integral to the "imaginary relationship of individuals to their real conditions of existence," to quote Louis Althusser (1971, 162). As Althusser shows, individuals are always *in* ideology. "There is no practice except by and in an ideology" (164), just as there is no practice except by and in time. While there is no way to step outside of time and its corresponding ideology, there is the possibility of moving among and across different ideological constructions of time to explore their various structures and social ramifications. Discourses of nostalgia, progress, destiny, capitalist expansion, and political process each have their own temporal logic. These discourses come together dialogically within early Mexican American literature, where discourses of time are refracted so that no single form of time constitutes a stable anchor or "real" time from which to view the others. I draw again from Sandoval's (2000) concept of differential consciousness to apply it specifically to time consciousness. Mexican American authors practice what Sandoval describes as a "semiotic" methodology; they read the way that time signifies in relation to power.

Early Mexican American writing moves across and between forms of time through narrative form and through the hermeneutics of textual recovery that bind past and future together. *In the Mean Time* participates in the hermeneutics of literary recovery or in what Avery Gordon calls "making common cause" with the subject of study. Also addressing the inadequacy of postmodern epistemology, Gordon writes, "Making common cause means that our encounters must strive to go beyond the fundamental alienation of turning social relations into just the things we know and toward our own reckoning with how we are in these stories, with how they change us" (2008, 45). While being intellectually rigorous, *In the Mean Time* is also invested in the texts and authors it explores; its methodology comes as much from the primary sources as from the literary theory of the twentieth and twenty-first centuries.

I look specifically to texts that engage historical narrative and narratives of capitalist modernization because they tug at the seams of homogenous, linear time and highlight the disunity of temporal experience for Mexican Americans in the late nineteenth and early twentieth centuries. For example, Ruiz de Burton quips that U.S. law works to "unsettle" California (1992, 84); Otero describes Anglo Western heroes as savage impediments to progress; *Caballero* contains narrative digressions into a violent future anterior; and De Zavala fights to save the Alamo from "capitalist syndicates" (1996, 46). Each of these rhetorical moves reconstitutes time as something other than a linear progression into the (better) future. While the texts maintain a dual focus on history (the past) and progress (the future), the authors' elite status also granted them access to U.S. political structures. Ruiz de Burton and Otero leveled a strong critique of Washington politics, while Adina De Zavala and Jovita González were involved in local politics, particularly through their participation in historical preservation and education. These two Tejana authors also interrogate the relation between patriarchy and patriotism, a relation that would return to haunt their position within the project of textual recovery. The writing I examine brings us into contact with temporal others, with specters that trouble the distinction between past, present, and future through differential movement across multiple ideological formations of time. Differential time consciousness is accessible through recovery and as recovery, particularly when recovery projects exceed the bounds of a contestation paradigm and explore the multiple registers and social positions of the texts and people they recover.

Writing Time

In the Mean Time engages with early Mexican American authors as producers rather than as objects of analysis, and with a cue from their writing, *In the Mean Time*'s structure can be read a number of ways. Each chapter demonstrates that resolution within linear, progressive time is inadequate—in the form of political inclusion, economic restitution, or even historical revision—because progressive time is itself an instrument of colonization. The authors I explore appear chronologically in this book, according to their birth and death dates, but that is only one way of imagining their temporal position. In another sense *In the Mean Time* is recursive because the subject matter moves from the 1870s to the 1900s, then back in time to the 1830s. At the same time it oscillates between novels and nonfiction histories of the Southwest, between canonical and less read texts of Mexican American literary recovery. In the spirit of differential consciousness, the chapters can be used separately to engage with different aspects of U.S. temporal colonization in the Southwest. Taken together, though, they form a cohesive network of strategies for navigating the U.S. colonization of time.

The first two chapters focus on the material forces at work in U.S. temporal colonization. New economies in the late nineteenth and early twentieth centuries manipulated Mexican Americans' time as devalued capital when Anglo immigrants defrauded Mexican Americans of their land and installed systems of wage labor. Federal politics also destabilized local political processes in the Southwest to classify Mexican Americans as sociologically underdeveloped and thus justify their political and economic disenfranchisement.

Chapter 1 opens with an exploration of Ruiz de Burton's *The Squatter and the Don* to historically situate temporal colonization of Mexican America through the capitalist expansion of railroads and their homogenization of U.S. time. *The Squatter and the Don* is especially adept in its expression of the material colonization of time by U.S. political and industrial institutions. The novel displays and interrogates multiple forms of time, through what Bakhtin (1981) calls "dialogism"—the novelistic interplay of distinct voices. For example, Californio land loss is presented through the rhetoric of both naturalistic decline and capitalist design. Likewise, various social constructions of time such as destiny, progress, evolution, and tradition come into contact as squatters, Californios, monopoly capitalists, and investment capitalists interact. The novel's focus on economy and its initial recovery as a tale of economic dispossession and contestation make it an important foundational text for the project of Mexican American literary recovery and thus for the critical project of *In the Mean Time*. Modern temporality's homogeneity is the basis for a temporal economy, where time is a reified commodity with uneven exchange value for Mexican Americans. As the Californios' land loses value, their time becomes less valuable as well. The economy of time extends beyond capitalist discourse, though, when it is represented in legalistic discourse throughout the novel. *The Squatter and the Don* exposes the failure of a U.S. legal system that has become entangled in a capitalist economy where money can buy votes and court rulings.

The Squatter and the Don's initial recovery by Rosaura Sánchez and Beatrice Pita as a contestatory novel likewise situates it in a temporal economy of justice. In this system cultural and literary recovery attempt to restore what was lost in the colonial process of historical erasure. Recovered texts contest the social, political, and economic domination of their historical context, while literary recovery projects contest similar types of domination in the period of recovery. But recovered texts are never univocal or purely contestatory. *The Squatter and the Don* is a paradigmatic text for the problems of recovery. It was composed by an elite Californiana who had significant social and political influence and who was clearly invested in classifying Californianas/os as racially white. Scholars such as José Aranda and Jesse Alemán have done much to trouble the idea of Ruiz de Burton's work as subaltern or anticipating a proletarian Chicana/o subject. As an artifact of literary recovery, the novel goes beyond critiquing the specific system of U.S. laws to disrupt the fundamental premise of a temporal economy of justice.

Chapter 2 moves to a more specific analysis of the way U.S. political processes manipulate linear time as progress through the writing of Miguel Antonio Otero, New Mexico's first Nuevomexicano territorial governor. Otero's three-term governorship took place at the turn of the century, squarely in the Progressive Era, when U.S. progress was being delinked from western expansion and reformulated as a process of reform and modernization. Despite the shifting focus on progress as a form of time rather than a spatial movement, Mexican Americans continued to be excluded from U.S. modernity. Otero's work demonstrates this clearly because he was so heavily invested in modernizing New Mexico to gain political enfranchisement. His writing highlights the interplay of modernity, modernization, and modernism in colonizing the U.S. Southwest. Modernization is the material process that fills modernity's empty, temporal structure with Euro-American values. The United States places itself at the forefront of modernity by valorizing its own social, economic, and technological *modernization* as the newest, best, and most advanced forms of human behavior. Progressive politics' emphasis on modernization reinforced U.S. modernity's racializing forms of time that organized people hierarchically, as more or less advanced within the same historical moment. Literary modernism worked in tandem with modernity's racialized time when Anglo-American writers aestheticized Nuevomexicanos as slow, unintelligent, and unresourceful in their escapist regional literature.

Otero wrote against modernism's regionalist nostalgia and U.S. modernity's corresponding political rhetoric of underdevelopment. As a politician, he tried to appease demands for territorial modernization by reforming corrupt political practices and promoting technological and economic investment in the territory. Otero's work and writing show that even when Mexican Americans align themselves with the ideological values of U.S. modernity—privileging newness, promoting capitalist exchange and technological advancement, and defending legislative and judicial processes—U.S. modernity's underlying linear, progressive temporality works as a tool of exclusion to deny colonized subjects participation in the present.

The final two chapters develop a more theoretical engagement with Mexican American authors' response to temporal colonization. I flesh out the argument that Sandoval's differential consciousness is a temporal methodology. Mexican American literature moves differentially across multiple forms of time to explore social, political, and economic power structures in the United States. Each discourse provides a vantage point from which another discourse's temporal ideology can be dismantled. Differential time consciousness is open-ended and dialogic rather then a teleological process of dialectic synthesis. The heterogeneity of Mexican American literary inheritance, I suggest, is grounded in heterogeneous forms of time, and differential movement between them charts a path toward what Chicana theorists have described as a third space (time) that defies the dichotomy between presence and absence.

Chapter 3 looks to Adina De Zavala's preservation work as an archival iteration of differential movement across forms of time. It develops an analysis of the ways that historical preservation and literary recovery must participate in the capitalist market to acquire and distribute historical material. Thus, literary recovery and historical preservation become embroiled in abstract forms of homogenous, empty time that support capitalist exchange, particularly through the concept of debt or indebtedness. De Zavala's preservation of the

Alamo exemplifies capitalism's alienating influence on historical preservation. Viewing the building as San Antonio's communal inheritance, De Zavala tried to purchase it through her Daughters of the Republic of Texas chapter but was ultimately overpowered by the capitalist vision of her primary donor, Clara Driscoll. Along with her supporters, Driscoll saw philanthropic donations as an investment in San Antonio's aesthetic appeal and racialized narrative of Anglo Texan superiority. De Zavala's later preservation work, including her book *History and Legends of the Alamo* (1996), resists the commodity fetishization of historical icons by emphasizing the past's heterogeneity and material specificity above and against its abstract exchange value. Her methodology is relevant to contemporary literary recovery and archival formation because scholars continue to recover and preserve history within the temporal economy of capitalist exchange. In this system Mexican American history and intellectual production—like Mexican American land and labor—are devalued through processes of unequal exchange. Archive formation specifically connects alienating capitalist forms of time to psychoanalytic developmental forms of time in ethnic identity construction. *History and Legends* creates an intertextual dialogue with the past that does not try to restore temporal cohesion but instead brings multiple voices together, including those entirely outside modernity's purview, like ghosts and other folk personages. De Zavala's work creates a relationship of responsibility to those not present and those denied presence by modern ideological formations of time.

Chapter 4 explores to the work of Jovita González, including *Caballero*, the historical novel she coauthored with Margaret Eimer, to examine differential time consciousness's dialogic structure. *Caballero* mines the temporal rupture of Anglo colonization and traces alternate paths of cultural inheritance for Mexican Americans. The novel demonstrates that both Tejano patriarchal tradition and U.S. modernity are exclusionary, linear constructions of time, though the two forms of time are at odds with each other throughout the novel. González and Eimer dialogically juxtapose tradition and modernity to reveal their colonial implications in the lives of women and peons. The characters' interpersonal exchange of social memories also undermines hegemonic constructions of cultural memory to disrupt the idea of a reified cultural identity based in a shared past. These temporal practices place Mexican Americans not outside of U.S. modernity but always moving across multiple forms of time in a way that exposes time's ideological implications. *Caballero* shows how historical conditions circumscribe women's ability to be desiring subjects but also how differential movement opens up a time-space for the women's and peons' desiring subjectivity.

I extend the analysis of *Caballero*'s differential time consciousness into the hermeneutics of textual recovery. When the novel was published in 1996, it was framed by two competing interpretations of the text as accommodationist or contestatory, paradigms that reflect early debates over the recovery of Ruiz de Burton's and Otero's work as well. But, like tradition and progress, contestation and accommodation rely on linear paradigms that project a false unity onto complex, contradictory forms of time. To move differentially across multiple ideological forms of time, recovery work must be dialogic rather than dialectic, not a closed, linear process of synthesis but an open-ended, intertextual engagement.

The afterword moves to the Chicana/o Renaissance of the 1970s, 1980s, and early 1990s, before the Latina/o literary recovery movement published premovement writers. Thus, it explores the spectral inheritance of early Mexican American literature for a generation that did not have the opportunity to read it. I trace Chicana/o literature's recursive relationship to nonlinear narrative and its disruption of U.S. modernity. Chicana/o literature during and after the Chicano Movement also reconstitutes time as a socially constructed matrix through which characters and readers move. The afterword also looks to broader trends in Chicana/o cultural imagining, like the concept of Aztlán or the recuperation of *corridos*, as cultural origin stories to highlight the way that Chicana/o writers creatively engage with the past. Their resistant temporal methodology is not just a consequence but also a recurrence of early literature that was largely lost to late twentieth-century authors and readers. As in Alejandro Morales's (1992) *The Rag Doll Plagues*, inheritance becomes a repetition rather than a lineage.

CHAPTER I

Temporal Colonization

Getting Railroaded in *The Squatter and the Don*

Before 1872, the year in which María Amparo Ruiz de Burton's *The Squatter and the Don* opens, the United States had no standardized time system. Towns and counties throughout the country kept time according to their solar meridian. Wisconsin had thirty-eight time zones; Chicago trains ran on Columbus, Ohio, time, which was nineteen minutes different from Chicago time; and the clocks in New York, Boston, and Philadelphia were all several minutes apart.[1] In 1872 U.S. railroad systems tentatively accepted a proposal by Charles Dowd that created standardized time zones to more effectively coordinate train schedules. During this transitional phase railroad standard time coexisted with local time, and railroads created indexes so that passengers could convert their local times to railroad time and back again. Thus, just as Ruiz de Burton's iconic nineteenth-century novel, *The Squatter and the Don*, begins its narrative, time is literally in flux throughout the nation.

By 1885, the year of the novel's publication, a revised version of the time zones successfully replaced the Dowd plan. This time the railroads did not provide conversion indexes for passengers. James W. Carey explains that the new plan's author, William Frederick Allen, "recommended that the railroads abandon the practice of providing a minute index and that they simply adopt standard time for regulating their schedules and allow communities and institutions to adjust to the new time in any manner they chose" (1992, 322). While there were some noted protests, the new system of time was adopted across the United States within months. By becoming invisible, railroad time became U.S. time.[2]

Embedded in the context of this monumental transformation to U.S. time-keeping, *The Squatter and the Don* pushes against the colonizing ubiquity of homogenous time. The book's subtitle, "A Novel Descriptive of Contemporary Occurrences in California," doubly emphasizes time. "Contemporary" indicates a relationship of things that are coeval, or existing in a shared present, and it modifies "occurrences," which likewise places emphasis on the temporal aspect of an event (contrast it with the word "situations," which would have placed the emphasis on space). Add to this the subtitle's reference to a "novel," the genre in which "time, as it were, thickens, takes on flesh [and] becomes artistically visible," according to Mikhail Bakhtin, and you have a book about time in California (1981, 84). The "contemporary occurrences" described by *The Squatter and the Don* reveal disparate forms of U.S. modern time that coalesce to disenfranchise Mexican Americans.

The Squatter and the Don adroitly navigates the U.S. national "imagined community" by disrupting the homogenous empty time that Benedict Anderson (2006) would later describe as a hallmark of national identity. In contrast to Anderson, Thomas Allen describes national time as a "shared network or web of timing . . . [that] is constructed out of the various uses individuals make of time" (2008, 11). But both Anderson's and Allen's descriptions of national time neglect the role of colonization. The development of standard time was a slow, uneven process of subordinating some forms of time to others. *The Squatter and the Don* exposes the politics that structure U.S. modernity as a colonial practice of subordinating local forms of time to national and capitalist time. I draw on Bakhtin's assertion that multiple forms of time come together dialogically in a novel (he calls novelistic forms of time "chronotopes" and asserts that they are closely related to genre structure) (1981, 250). The dialogic juxtaposition of forms of time in *The Squatter and the Don* allows readers to move across different ways of thinking about community, economy, nationalism, and political processes to question temporal homogeneity and, consequently, temporal hegemony.

The dialogic interplay of forms of time in *The Squatter and the Don* reveals the colonial force of U.S. modernity's particular iterations of homogenous, empty, linear time in the form of monopoly capitalism and Manifest Destiny. As the novel critiques the big four railroads' monopoly capitalism, the abstract time of the financial market appears cold and disorienting in contrast to the characters' localized, communal experiences of time. *The Squatter and the Don*'s critique of monopoly capitalism is in many ways a critique of capitalist time—of the way that capitalism produces time as empty and homogenous to assign it a market value that can be manipulated, regulated, and predicted. The U.S. temporal economy figures exchange values not just for material goods but also for people's social and political interactions. U.S. colonial forms of time work in consort with the homogenizing force of monopoly capitalism to racialize Californio land owners and dispossess them of their wealth and status.

The Squatter and the Don brings together a number of situated and often contradictory forms of time, including legalistic discourse, romance, economic transaction, and social invective, to highlight the ideological underpinnings of U.S. colonization. The novel also has a double ending—romantic closure followed by a denunciation of political corruption—that leaves it unresolved and open to an unknowable future. Its form and content undermine universalizing abstract ideas about time as empty and homogenous or linear and progressive. The novel moves across different forms of time within dominant U.S. discourses to coordinate Mexican Americans within and against U.S. modernity. Each discourse provides a vantage point from which another discourse's temporal ideology can be dismantled.

Ruiz de Burton's novel of contemporary events describes the financial ruin of the Alamar family when Anglo-American squatters shoot their cattle while the Alamar land grant is under legal dispute. At the same time a proposed Texas Pacific Railroad would make the squatters and the Alamars alike wealthy by joining their land in San Diego to the Gulf Coast. The novel's plot revolves around several romances, including the courtship of Mercedes Alamar by Clarence Darrell, the chivalrous stock-trading son of a notorious squatter; the marriage of Gabriel Alamar, Don Mariano's oldest son, to Lizzie Mechlin, the daughter of their wealthy Anglo neighbors; a similar marriage between

Elvira Alamar and George Mechlin; and a budding romance between the don's youngest son, Victoriano, and Clarence's little sister, Alice. The plot is interwoven with moments of social invective against Central Pacific Railroad monopolists and the congressmen they bribed in the late nineteenth century. The novel narrates a history of U.S. injustice against Californios in what Lene M. Johannessen calls a "pedagogical subtext" that "targets an Anglo-American audience" (2008, 73). Chicana/o scholars, including Albert Camarillo (1984) and Rosaura Sánchez (1995), attribute a nascent ethnic identification among the Californio community to this period as a response not only to land loss but also to the racialization of Californios by U.S. invaders. *The Squatter and the Don*, in particular, is an interesting case study in this process because its emphasis on Californio whiteness belies an anxiety about U.S. racialization of elite Mexican Americans. While the novel is frequently read as a protest against the U.S. colonization of Californio land, it must also be read as an attempt to grapple with the U.S. colonization of time, because time is the medium through which racialization occurs.[3]

After a lengthy discussion with Clarence about the abuse of land laws that has led to Californio dispossession, Don Mariano says, "I am afraid there is no remedy for us native Californians. We must sadly fade and pass away. The weak and helpless are always trampled in the throng. We must sink, go under, never to rise. If Americans had been friendly to us, and helped us with good, protective laws, our fate would have been different. But to legislate us into poverty is to legislate us into our graves" (Ruiz de Burton 1992, 165). The beginning of Don Mariano's statement parallels Anglo-American imperialist nostalgia.[4] The temporal logic of imperialist nostalgia works by placing a colonized group of people so far in the past that they figuratively disappear from the present. And, as with Manifest Destiny, imperialist nostalgia imagines a colonized people's demise as fated and eminent. Within the United States, imperialist nostalgia frequently aligns with Manifest Destiny through the trope of the "vanishing Indian." One of the best literary examples of imperialist nostalgia in California is Helen Hunt Jackson's (1884) *Ramona*, with which *The Squatter and the Don* has been compared repeatedly.[5] As the "weak and helpless" Californios sink, "never to rise" again, Don Mariano plays to the trope of imperialist nostalgia by softening an image of social Darwinism through the romance of loss.

Rhetorically, imperialist nostalgia absolves colonizers of their responsibility for colonial violence, depicting the demise of colonized people as natural and fated in order to ignore the realities of genocide, political oppression, and economic dispossession. The second half of Don Mariano's statement, however, exposes the inner workings of imperialist nostalgia by squarely placing the blame for Mexican American disenfranchisement on U.S. legislators. *The Squatter and the Don* points out that it is not Californios' Manifest Destiny to disappear in the wake of U.S. colonization. Rather, U.S. laws are specifically designed to rob Californios of their land and force them into poverty. In an 1869 letter to her friend and former statesman Mariano Vallejo, Ruiz de Burton writes, "El Manifest Destiny no es otra cosa que 'Manifest Yankie trick'" (Sánchez and Pita 2001, 281). In the novel Don Mariano's discourse simultaneously acknowledges and refutes the rhetoric of U.S. western expansion. He revokes the epistemology of Manifest Destiny as a fated, divinely ordained process and places U.S. western expansion squarely in the realm of human political action. More important, these actions occur not in the past or in the divinely ordained future but in the present, with very real physical and material consequences for Californios. The novel's pedagogical element works to correct colonization's devastating disruption of Californio lives by demonstrating that the "destined" Californio demise was and still is preventable.

Industrial capitalist ideology constructs time as empty and homogenous in order to control the future—from train schedules to labor productivity to market fluctuations. Yet the U.S. desire to conquer time and the future predates the industrial boom of the nineteenth century and depends on another key feature of colonized time: its linearity. Linear time underlies narratives of progress and development. Writing about modernity's conception of history as the linear progression of events, Walter Mignolo explains, "History is based on what happened and not on what could have happened. Philosophy, though, is based on possible worlds and on always asking about the alternatives that have been left out by that which 'really happened.' In other words, 'historical reality' is not only what happened but also the possibilities that the facts of what happened negate" (2005, 29). Linear, progressive time allows colonizers to narrowly define and control the past—"what really happened"—but it also allows colonial powers to project their dominance into the future. Mignolo's critique of modernity's linear, progressive time is particularly interesting if we apply it to the U.S. ideology of Manifest Destiny, which excludes alternate possibilities for the future, not just the past. Manifest Destiny makes the future present by imagining future events as having already happened. Indeed, John O'Sullivan uses the word "already" nine times in "Annexation," his 1845 article that first introduced the term "Manifest Destiny," when he imagines both Texas and California as "ours [a]lready" eight months before the inception of the U.S.-Mexico War (5). By constructing the United States as always already at the forefront of development (social, technological, political, etc.), nineteenth-century Anglo-American texts mark the United States as the epitome of modernity. The linearity of modern time makes this U.S. form of time both homogenous and exclusionary. The nation progresses forever into the future as the newness of modernity's present is projected onto a future newness; its destiny, made manifest, continues into a future of perpetual growth and expansion.

The ideology of Manifest Destiny erased the material reality of U.S. colonization by making it a divinely ordained imperative rather than the result of social and political design. However, the political process of western expansion depended on social systems of coloniality that hierarchically categorize race and ethnicity. Manifest Destiny racialized time by claiming that conquered peoples belong to the past while conquering Anglo-Americans or western Europeans are harbingers of the future. In an 1824 letter to William Ludlow, Thomas Jefferson described the United States as containing bands of progress from the "savages of the Rocky Mountains," to "our own semi-barbarous citizens, the pioneers," to "as yet, [the] most improved state in our seaport towns," explaining that "this, in fact, is equivalent to a survey, in time, of the progress of man from the infancy of creation to present day" (qtd. in Allen 2008, 40–41). Sixty-nine years later Frederick Jackson Turner would reassert the link between anthropological theories of development and U.S. geography in his Frontier Thesis. Jefferson's and Turner's writing is part of a tradition that places Mexican Americans' and the far-western territories outside the temporal flow of modernity, perpetually in the past, and thus excluded from both the present and the future. *The Squatter and the Don* works to undermine the United States' racialized linkage of space and time by highlighting Californio presence.

Capitalist Time's Colonization of California

In situating Californios in the present, Ruiz de Burton's contemporary novel makes visible the material and the ideological process of temporal colonization in late nineteenth-century California. The 1851 California Land Act worked to "unsettle" Californio land grants, as Ruiz de Burton puts it, so that the newly acquired territory could be legally colonized by Anglo-American settlers (1992, 84). What counted as progress for U.S. legislators was retrograde for Californios, who believed they had already settled California in the eighteenth century. The new landscape of Anglo-American settlers and their accompanying economic systems also brought new conceptions of time to the region. While the railroads and other capitalist industries work to make time invisible and thus ubiquitous, *The Squatter and the Don*'s novelistic form highlights the constructed nature of time through a dialogic juxtaposition of various chronotopes. *The Squatter and the Don* moves across these forms of time to reveal each chronotope's ideological underpinnings and their relation to political and economic power in the United States.

Just as 1870s railroad time indexes coordinated multiple modes of time-keeping for passengers, the Alamars coordinate a network of times in their daily life, including spiritual, economic, organic, political, and mechanistic modes of keeping time. While participating in the 1870s California ranching economy, Don Mariano reflects an already variegated conception of time that predates U.S. colonization. Measured, mechanical time had long been used in Spanish California by the mission system, where mission bells were used to strictly regulate Indian labor. Eulalia Pérez, an overseer at the California mission, San Gabriel, describes the convergence of different forms of time in an 1877 interview with historian Thomas Savage. She outlines the schedule of Indian labor according to clock time, explaining that girls at the mission would go to mass and breakfast, then unload *carretas* until eleven o'clock, eat lunch at one, and work until sunset (qtd. in Bebee and Senkewicz 2006, 107–8). Her description aptly characterizes the interconnection of spiritual time, organic or natural time, and clock time because tasks were regulated by the clock but ended at sunset and included time specifically reserved for worship. The church calendar also created a temporality that was *full*, in contrast to the scientific, industrial conception of *empty* time. The Catholic calendar of saint's days, as well as the Lenten season, Advent, and Ordinary Time, creates a temporality of remembrance and connection across time, where days are filled with spiritual and historical meaning.

During the process of Mexican secularization in 1833, the mission system was "sublated" by the rancho or hacienda system, as Sánchez describes, which "displace[d] the mission as the central space of production" (1995, 142). Forms of time from the missions continued as residual chronotopes, just as the Alamars continue to practice the Catholic faith in their new U.S. national context. But neither the Alamars' Catholicism nor their participation in a semifeudal economy place them in Benedict Anderson's premodern temporal "simultaneity of past and present through acts of remembrance and reenactment" with "no conception of history as an endless chain of cause and effect" (2006, 23, 26). Indeed, as with Eulalia Pérez's description of the mission system, clock time and spiritual time coexist in the Alamars' Christmas celebration, when the mantle clock strikes midnight and "at the same time an alter was disclosed to view, tastefully decorated in the Roman Catholic style" (Ruiz de Burton 1992, 303).[6] Likewise, Don Mariano's economic impulses stem from an understanding of the soil and climate, gained over time through his participation in the localized organic time of planting, growing, and harvesting. He advises the newly arrived squatters to plant vineyards, olives, and oranges—crops formerly grown by the missions—instead of wheat.

In addition to this already multiple, spiritual, and organic network of time, Don Mariano embraces the individualistic mechanical time of U.S. capitalism by wearing a watch (note that this is different from the communal mechanical time of mission bells). He examines his watch only once in the novel, during a snowstorm, and the events of this scene disclose a great deal about capitalism and mechanical time. Clarence Darrell has purchased the Alamars' cattle to keep them from being shot by Anglo-American homesteaders attempting to squat on the Alamars' land. But, when some of the cattle wander back to the Alamar rancho, Don Mariano, Victoriano, and their vaqueros try to drive the cattle back to Clarence's mining operation, where they will be used to feed the miners. In the middle of the night, a snowstorm envelops the men and the cattle they are driving. Don Mariano "sat up and looked around, but saw nothing. . . . He struck a light to look at his watch, for he had no idea what the hour might be. By the light he saw that his blankets seemed covered with flour" (Ruiz de Burton 1992, 278). The snow has obscured everything, including Don Mariano's sense of time. His spatial awareness is likewise affected when, the next day, he needs a pocket compass to find his way home (279). Scientific instrumentation for spatial and temporal orientation is necessary because Don Mariano and his men have no natural cues to guide them. The snow creates a time-space that is blank and uniform. But, unlike the celebrated time of scientific and national progress, the chronotopic blankness of the snow signals disorientation and devastation for a colonized people trying to embrace capitalist economies on uneven ground with their Anglo-American colonizers. Don Mariano catches pneumonia, Victoriano's legs are paralyzed, and most of the cattle die. While Don Mariano's watch is a symbol of his status, it also signals the loss of other temporal markers. The personal timepiece signifies a disconnection from communal and ecological time and is necessary only in an alienating, blank landscape.

The squatters on the Alamars' land also operate within a number of temporal constructions. They too depend on the land for their livelihood, but their form of time, like their crop system, is a secondary colonial importation that wreaks havoc on the social cohesion of Californio society. As harbingers of Manifest Destiny, the squatters epitomize the U.S. desire to colonize the future. William Darrell exclaims in the opening chapter, "I had better take time by the forelock and get a good lot of land in the Alamar grant" (Ruiz de Burton 1992, 57). Darrell wants to control time by rushing headlong into the future, where he projects himself as a prosperous farmer. His future focus impoverishes his understanding of the past, as his genteel wife explains. Darrell had already staked claims on land in the Napa and Sonoma Valleys, putting a great deal of labor into a homestead only to have his claims rejected when the land under dispute was awarded to its original Californio owner. William tells his wife, "No use in crying over spilt milk, eh?" but she corrects him: "Let us cry for the *spilt milk* by all means, if by doing so we can learn how to avoid spilling any more. . . . Much wisdom is learnt through tears, but none by forgetting our lessons" (55). But William Darrell cannot meaningfully remember the past, because he believes there is no profit in it. His future focus is an economically motivated tool of colonization.

Later in the novel Darrell becomes embroiled in the schemes of his fellow squatters to oust the Alamars from their land. The rest of the Darrell family is friendly with the Alamars and prefer to purchase the land outright. They call the room where William Darrell meets with fellow squatters "the colony . . . because the talk there is always about locating, or surveying, or fencing land—always land—as it would be in a new colony" (Ruiz de Burton 1992, 215). As the family becomes concerned with Darrell's behavior, William Darrell himself becomes internally conflicted, yet too proud to amend his actions. As Darrell becomes more entrenched in his squatter behavior, mechanical time metaphorically disrupts his social interactions. Instead of spending time with his family, he smokes outside "like an overturned locomotive which had run off its track," capturing the mechanical, though derailed, time of a train. Later, unable to interact with his son Clarence, William Darrell responds by "not looking at anyone's face excepting that of the clock on the chimney mantel" (216). The mechanistic clock disrupts communal relations by replacing the faces of Darrell's family with its own face at the same time that its placement on the mantel works to internalize homogenous time's temporal economy within the domestic space.

Despite the Alamars' and the squatters' different networks of time, there is a sense in the novel that the two groups can coexist, especially if the squatters take Don Alamar's advice about planting different crops. As long as the squatters stop shooting the Alamars' cattle, their economic systems will be compatible, which is perhaps why Rosaura Sánchez and Beatrice Pita collapse both the squatters and the don under the rubric of "Individual Entrepreneur" in their schema for the novel (1992, 27). Though adaptable and innovative, the don and the squatters depend on land and its corresponding organic rhythms of planting and cattle raising. Likewise, all the San Diegans whose livelihood depends on land suffer at the hands of the railroad, an entity that, in contrast to William Darrell, really does control time within the novel.

Unlike haciendados, settlers, and squatters, the Central Pacific Railroad is able to fully divorce its existence from local organic time. It exists in the measured homogenous time of clocks. The railroads' homogenous time can be scheduled and regulated like the empty pages of a date book. Maureen Perkins's describes the modern calendar or date book in contrast to earlier liturgical calendars and almanacs as a "blank slate, representing the future rather than the past. It is [the] Lockean promise of a future onto which any intentions may be inscribed" (2001, 29). The railroad system's future focus reveals its investment in the idea of progress and its emphasis on forward motion. The hegemony of railroad time is most apparent in the novel when Don Mariano, Mr. Holman, and Mr. Mechlin go to San Francisco to speak with Governor Stanford about the possibility of a rail line extending to San Diego. After forcing the visitors to wait two hours, Stanford tells them, "I . . . can only give you half an hour" (Ruiz de Burton 1992, 290). When Stanford finally responds clearly to the men's question, he tells them, "No, perhaps for the present San Diego will *not* have a railroad," and they ask him, "What do you call *for the present*? How long?" (291). These actions demonstrate that Stanford, and by extension the railroad, is in control of time. He defines the time of their interaction and the very structure of the present for San Diegans. Stanford also repeatedly looks at his watch during the meeting. While he regulates and controls time, Stanford looks to an external chronometer, as if his watch is actually the regulatory device ticking away and dictating his schedule. These moves shore up both the irony and the hegemony of railroad time, particularly when we remember that Stanford's watch is set to a standardized time implemented by the railroad company itself. The duration of the "present," in which Stanford denies San Diego a rail line, is actually forever. Like the Treaty of Guadalupe Hidalgo's "mean time," Stanford's ability to control time installs economic dependency and disenfranchises Mexican Americans politically. Stanford's eternal present parallels and inverts U.S. modernity's perpetual newness. The scene indicates that Stanford controls duration—"How long?"—at the same time that it demonstrates the way Californios were denied presence within a U.S. industrial economy.

The railroad's temporality is made possible by its economic disconnection from any religious, organic, or cyclical time. At one point Stanford tells Mr. Holman, "You see we are not engaged in the fruit-growing business. We build railroads to transport freight and passengers. We do not care what or who makes the freights we carry" (Ruiz de Burton 1992, 290). Even Stanford's grammatical placement of the word "what" before "who" emphasizes that the economy of the railroad is reified and mechanized, concerned with commodities rather than people and run entirely on standard time. Forced into a homogenous, measured form of time, Mr. Holman later responds, "Much as we would like to await your pleasure, we cannot arrest the march of time. Time goes on, and as it slips by, ruin approaches us" (292). In this way the railroad monopolists' economic colonization of California depends as much on their control of time as it does on their control of space. Whereas in the older economic system, Mariano and his Anglo neighbors might have weathered difficult financial times by awaiting the next season, when their crops would be healthier or their cattle more plentiful, the constant forward movement of time within the new industrial capitalist system allows them no recovery. It is, in fact, their heavy investment in land that condemns them because their land is worthless in this capitalist economy without the presence of a railroad. The colonization of Californio land depends on the political and economic colonization of time.

Trading in Futures

The novel details capitalism's transformation of time—including the time of social and political interaction—into an exchange value that can be manipulated by political and economic powers even as it is held up as an external and equalizing resource (i.e., everyone has the same number of hours in a day). Interestingly, capitalist temporal hegemony is most visible in the novel's apparent hero. Clarence Darrell, the character most adept at using capitalist financial structures to his own advantage, is able to profit from empty homogenous time not by creating it but by manipulating it. In contrast to the squatters, the Alamars, and the Mechlins, Clarence Darrell's economic transactions leave him unscathed by the homogenous empty time that railroads helped to create and that they symbolize in the novel. Clarence thrives in a global financial economy by dominating the stock market. He succeeds by trading in futures. The railroad is able to divest the Alamars' and the squatters' land of its value by excluding them from the circuit of transportation and thus the circulation of goods, but Clarence manages to bypass this problem by focusing on the exchange value of goods rather than their more spatially dependent use value.

Capitalist trade was originally based on arbitrage—buying goods in one place, transporting them, and then selling them in a place where prices were higher. If the resale profit was greater than the cost of transportation, then the arbitrage trader succeeded. Carey points out that arbitrage is based in space because prices depend on location and transportation. The railroads equalized this trade system by making transportation fast and cheap, reducing the difference in regional prices throughout the nation. In *The Squatter and the Don*, the railroad controls this system entirely by reshaping space through the access it grants or denies to different regions—hence San Diego's investment in building the Texas Pacific Railroad in the first place. But while railroads reduce regional price differences, they still operate in a system of trade dependent on space. In contrast, communication technologies like the telegraph make communication virtually instantaneous, and thus, Carey explains, "it shifts speculation from space to time, from arbitrage to futures" (1992, 315). He goes on to say, "In a certain sense, the telegraph invented the future as a new zone of uncertainty and a new region of practical action" (316). The shift to an economy based in time rather than space marked the rise of investment capitalism made possible by new communication technology.[7] Clarence makes the correlation apparent as he utilizes the telegraph to communicate with his broker, Hubert Haverly, who likewise uses the telegraph to trade Clarence's money.

The temporality of Clarence's economic exchange is both dependent on and exterior to the forward-moving homogenous empty time created by railroad monopolists. His trading is marked by simultaneity, in which the future exists for speculation in the present and actions are often nonlinear—where, as Carey writes, "the futures trader often sells before he buys or buys and sells simultaneously" (1992, 317). This is the financial realm in which Clarence acts and in which he makes his millions. Unlike William Darrell, who erroneously imagines his future prosperity without understanding the past, Clarence's economic system calls for a consideration of multiple networks of time at once. His command of multiple forms of capitalist time—ranching, mining, stock trading, and so on—is what makes Clarence paradoxically both the liberator and the oppressor of the novel. He is able to move across different temporalities, but he uses that ability for personal financial gain.

His speculation is the ultimate commodification of time. By the novel's close every significant character has become dependent on Clarence and his money. Mercedes Alamar marries Clarence, and they bring her mother and sisters to San Francisco with them. Gabriel, Victoriano, and George all depend on Clarence's plan to open a bank in San Francisco, where they will work as tellers, and Clarence purchases the Alamars' land and the Darrells' Alameda homestead.

As the key to *The Squatter and the Don*'s romantic resolution, Clarence Darrell is both seductive and dangerous. Jesse Alemán points out that "the immateriality of Clarence's material possessions highlights perhaps the most profound form of narrative amnesia: the novel tries to forget that Clarence is an Anglo profiting from Manifest Destiny" (2002, 69). In the end Clarence buys all of the Alamars' land for four dollars an acre, even though it is a "high price for land in this country" because he can afford to wait for land prices to rise and "double the price paid" (Ruiz de Burton 1992, 332). The money from this sale will allow Gabriel Alamar to invest in Clarence's San Francisco bank as a partner. Thus Clarence profits doubly from San Diego's decline, as Gabriel reinvests Clarence's money back into their bank venture. Clarence's ability to work outside the realm of linear, progressive time or, more accurately, his ability to make linear, progressive time work on his behalf sets him up as a possible avatar, a projection of Ruiz de Burton's own desire for capitalist financial gain. After all, the Burtons did participate in capitalist ventures, and after her husband's death Ruiz de Burton continued to seek investment capital for the development of her land in Baja California (though she was not particularly successful). Thus Clarence's financial success may symbolize what the author could have achieved if not for gender and racial constraints. His business savvy within the novel reveals Ruiz de Burton's own economic adroitness and, more importantly, her capacity to think and move outside of linear, progressive time.

On the other hand, Clarence's manipulation of linear time signifies something more sinister in the way that it produces economic dependence for the Alamars. Latin American dependency theory argues that colonial and neocolonial capitalist powers produce underdevelopment in Latin America and the Global South. Nineteenth-century capitalist (and Marxist) global economic theories posited universal stages of economic development through which each nation would pass on its path toward economic growth and enlightenment. Like sociological scales of development that equate one ethnoracial group's present with another's past, economic development theories deny what Johannes Fabian (2002) calls coevalness between "developing" and "developed" nations. Latin American dependency theory, in contrast, argues that colonial and neocolonial capitalism intentionally produces underdevelopment in colonial and postcolonial nations to bolster the economic growth of the Global North.[8] *The Squatter and the Don* shows the same processes working within a single nation, across regional and ethnic differences. While ideas like Manifest Destiny and imperialist nostalgia relegate colonized peoples to the sociological past, capitalist dependency relegates them to poverty in the present. Clarence signifies an international flow of capital through his investment in the stock market and his business travel to Mexico, South America, and Europe, but his transactions also create regional economic dependency for the Alamars. While the railroad monopoly produces an underdeveloped San Diego as the inadvertent result of its market hoarding, Clarence's financial growth *depends* on that underdevelopment. The depressed land value in San Diego allows him to buy large tracts, and the impoverished Californios become his "partners," both economically and romantically.

Even though futures trading posits a nonlinear simultaneity of stock purchase and speculation in contrast to the linear, progressive time of industrial capitalism, it nonetheless depends on modernity's underlying temporal homogeneity. Futures speculation necessitates a standardized and abstracted sense of time to make predictions about the market. Discussing forms of time in market fluctuation and growth, William H. Sewell explains, "No other institutional complex in the history of the world has pivoted so much on a process of universal abstraction as has capitalism" (2008, 533). While railroads may have created standardized time zones to avoid train wrecks, stock markets were equally dependent on this synchronized time system to coordinate financial speculation and futures trading. Clarence's capitalist transactions deepen, rather than overturn, the grip of homogenous time on social structures within the novel.

One of the most overt threats of colonial dependency within the novel appears in Gabriel Alamar's descent into wage labor. While Clarence is absent, Gabriel loses his position as a teller at a San Francisco bank (not the bank Clarence proposes they open together). Gabriel is unable to find more "gentlemanly work," because of prejudice against "Spanish Californians," and takes a job as a bricklayer for two dollars a day (Ruiz de Burton 1992, 317). Thus, his body and its labor power become regulated by mechanical time. His reification and commodification come to a head when he is crushed by a hod full of bricks. While traveling to the hospital, Gabriel must wait for a procession of wealthy socialites to pass on their way to a reception in Nob Hill. Unknowingly, George and Clarence comment on the scene from a carriage on the other side of the procession, telling their driver that the sick passenger they see should be allowed to pass the procession. "'Yes sir; but he is a hod carrier who fell down and hurt himself. I suppose he'll die before he gets to the hospital,' said the driver indifferently as if a hod carrier was more or less of no consequence. 'The [socialites'] carriages must pass first, the police says'" (321). The scene discredits any egalitarian representations of homogenous time—the idea that we all have the same twenty-four hours in a day—to show that the commodification of time creates inequity, a situation where the minutes it takes for a wealthy socialite to cross the street are valued above the minutes needed to save a day laborer's fleeting life.

The scene at the intersection is, in fact, an intersection of different forms of time. While the socialites' time halts both Clarence's and Gabriel's movement, Gabriel is stuck inside this stasis, whereas Clarence's stasis is a moment of observation. Clarence is looking and commenting during the traffic stop, and as soon as he recognizes Lizzie and Gabriel, he commences motion by leaving his carriage and walking over to Gabriel. Also important is the fact that the time differential between laborer and capitalist is enforced by the police, the symbol par excellence of state authority. The fear of Californio proletarianization that the novel displays is, in fact, a fear of falling into a particular temporality where Californios' time, like their land, is devalued through legal and economic manipulation.

The promise of integration that Mercedes's marriage to Clarence seems to offer—a social contract that brings the organic time of reproduction under the aegis of national productivity—is undermined by the novel's dialogic form.

Indeed, Clarence and Mercedes's hasty, anticlimactic wedding is supplanted by the image of a railroad king's silver wedding party in San Francisco. The silver wedding is a farce of marriage and social grace put on by the uncouth nouveau riche. The narrator describes it as Doña Josefa watches from afar while lamenting her husband's death, effectively inverting romantic closure. The narrative ending is further supplemented by a conclusion titled "Out with the Invader," which cites current events in a direct address invective against political and economic corruption. While the characters of *The Squatter and the Don* benefit from Clarence and Mercedes's marriage and the closure it brings to their financial hardship, the novel's form refuses closure. In this way its dialogism is more than an accumulation of different chronotopes; it is a heterogeneous comingling of time(s) that subverts any dialectic synthesis that could be read as progress.

Retroactive Law

As different forms of time comingle in the novel, capitalist time's infiltration of the political sphere is perhaps the greatest injustice exposed by *The Squatter and the Don*. The novel undermines imperialist nostalgic images of Californio decline by positioning Californios squarely in the presence of political and economic injustice. In fact, Ruiz de Burton's *Novel Descriptive of Contemporary Occurrences in California* is so contemporary that it discusses texts published in the very year of the novel's own publication. It references letters exchanged between Collis Huntington and David Colton that detail how the big four railroad magnates bribed Washington politicians in the 1870s.[9] These letters came to light only during a lawsuit that lasted from 1883 to 1885. Emphasizing Californio presence in the 1870s and 1880s, *The Squatter and the Don* works to unravel the temporal chicanery of Manifest Destiny by holding Anglo-Americans and the U.S. Congress accountable for their actions in the present.

The real problem for Californios is the marriage of Manifest Destiny's political ideology with capitalism's manipulation of time. The novel incorporates a number of legal documents into its presentation of California history, including the 1851 California Land Act, the Treaty of Guadalupe Hidalgo, and court evidence from the Colton case. It also creates fictional legal documents in a tragicomic episode, where corrupt lawyer Peter Roper and squatter John Gasbang buy a false land claim from Charles Hogsden and take over the Mechlin house. Alemán notes that the use of legal documents in the novel works dialogically; he states, "In the process of legitimating the narrative's historical critique, it de-legitimates the social function of legal rhetoric in general by emphasizing its pliability as a fictional discourse" (2000, 45). This pliability is specifically a temporal pliability. Just as Clarence's economy involves bending time (such as selling stock before buying it), legal actions throughout the novel remake the past for the sake of Anglo-American profit. Don Mariano and Clarence both refer to the 1851 California Land Act as a "retroactive" law (Ruiz de Burton 1992, 65, 97). Speaking to George Mechlin, Don Mariano says, "How could Mexico have foreseen then that when scarcely half a dozen years should have elapsed, the trusted conquerors would, *In Congress Assembled*, pass laws which were to be retroactive upon the defenseless, helpless, conquered people, in order to despoil them?" (65). Likewise, Gasbang and Roper steal the Mechlin house by claiming that it was part of a claim staked by Charles Hogsden, and they "deny that in the year of 1873, or at any other time before or after that date . . . the said James Mechlin ever purchased . . . the aforesaid property . . . ever built a house, or planted trees or resided on said property" (313).

Gasbang and Roper's fictional lawsuit and the real 1851 California Land Act expose the failure of a temporal economy within the U.S. justice system. The U.S. legal system's form of time projects a progressive temporal economy of dialectical resolution, where past injustices are corrected by new laws, where unlawful action is addressed with retribution (punishment) or restitution (financial compensation), and where social justice increases over time as a form of progress that mirrors the technological progress of private industry. *The Squatter and the Don* exposes the failure of a U.S. legal system entangled in the capitalist economy, where money can buy votes and court rulings. But the novel gestures beyond critiquing the specific system of U.S. law to critique the fundamental premise of a temporal economy. It brings into question the possibility of justice in a linear time of judicial progress because law does not act linearly. In the case of Californios, it acts retroactively, not just to take their land but to claim that it was never Californio land in the first place.

Allegorically, Clarence's wealth and union with Mercedes represent one possible Californio response to the U.S. colonization of California. While the novel contests the material loss of Californio land, it also argues for the continuation of Californio status through its insistence that Californio elites are racially white. As Alemán writes, "The novel ultimately argues for a new californio coloniality, one that consolidates californio whiteness with the whiteness of refined Northerners" (2002, 67). A number of scholars have discussed the problematics of Ruiz de Burton's insistence on Californio whiteness, particularly in relation to the novel's initial recovery as a resistance text.[10] But even as the novel makes a claim for Californio whiteness, it recognizes the historical impossibility of successful consolidation. Elvira Alamar's husband, George Mechlin, is shot in the hip by a squatter; Lizzie Mechlin's husband, Gabriel Alamar, is crushed by a hod full of bricks; and Alice Darrell's sweetheart, Victoriano Alamar, loses the use of his legs during the snowstorm. The three men in these allegorical consolidations of Anglo and Californio whiteness live, but all are crippled.

John Morán González reads Gabriel's banking venture with Clarence as a permutation of Californio claims to whiteness, explaining, "If by the novel's close Gabriel Alamar no longer can claim the patriarchal inheritance of the rancho as the eldest son of Don Mariano, as a banker he no longer must work as a hod carrier either. . . . Gabriel is able to convert a renewed class status into 'whiteness,' and 'whiteness' into 'white-collar'" (2010, 100). But, again, Clarence creates a system of dependence, as he alone becomes the path to whiteness and white-collar existence for all the Alamars. Even though the Alamar men escape the kind of wage-labor time scheme that Gabriel faced, as members of the white-collar professional class they form a deeply internalized sense of empty homogenous time that must be scheduled and regulated. Their proximity to Clarence's wealth as bank tellers will not grant them access to his form of economy or his temporality. Within the system of debt peonage that Californio elites had controlled before the U.S. invasion, Mexican patriarchs largely dictated the activities and thus the temporality of their families and their laborers. The inheritance that Gabriel loses, then, is more than land and money. It is the ability to maintain his own sense of time.

In the new Anglo-American economy, Californios are crushed by time just as Gabriel is crushed by his hod full of bricks. The novel's recovery has emphasized Ruiz de Burton's narrative interjection: "In that hod full of bricks not only his own sad experience was represented, but the *entire history* of the native Californians *of Spanish descent* was epitomized." If the hod represents history, then it is history that crushes elite Californios—namely, the history created by Anglo-Americans who "[say] that the native Spaniards are lazy and stupid and thriftless" (1992, 325). Anglo-American discourse places Californios outside the temporal flow of U.S. modernity in a perpetual sociological past of underdevelopment. Excluded from the temporality of U.S. progress, Californios are forced to inhabit the temporality assigned to them by the Treaty of Guadalupe Hidalgo, "the mean time." Gabriel Alamar exposes what "the mean time" actually meant for Californios. Lizzie repeatedly urges Gabriel to stop working as a mason because Clarence will come for them soon, but he tells her, "Yes, but *in the mean time* I must earn enough to pay our board" (320). In stark contrast to Benedict Anderson's "meanwhile" of national community (2006, 25), the Treaty of Guadalupe Hidalgo's "mean time" enacts a perpetual deferral of Mexican American inclusion to make time for the U.S. installation of long-term colonial dependency and economic underdevelopment.

Chicana/o Literature's Historical Romance

The novel's disruption of linear time is not confined to the time of the plot or its historical moment of production but reverberates across time to disrupt the hermeneutics of textual recovery as well. *The Squatter and the Don*'s 1992 recovery by Sánchez and Pita as a contestatory novel worked to situate the text in a temporal economy of justice, where its recovery might help to restore what was lost in the colonial process of historical erasure. Sánchez and Pita express this succinctly in their introduction: "The exclusionary dynamics of hegemonic culture erase minority discourses, silence denunciatory voices and leave tremendous lacunae in the history of marginalized groups that recovery projects and research are today compelled to fill" (48). Sánchez and Pita project this purpose onto *The Squatter and the Don* when they write, "There is also an implicit challenge in the novel, an interpellation of today's readers, as citizens, or as descendants of *californios*, to resist oppression, to slay the monster who has not ceased to be victorious" (49). However, recovered texts are never univocal. As José Aranda writes, "Ruiz de Burton serves as an object lesson in the complexities and contradictions in reconstructing literary history" (1998, 554). The complex and contradictory impulses (to borrow Aranda's apt title) of Ruiz de Burton's work led to a heated critical debate about her place in Chicana/o literary history.[11] *The Squatter and the Don* was composed by an elite Californiana who had significant social and political influence and who was clearly invested in classifying Californios as racially white at the same time that she contested U.S. social, legal, and economic systems. Scholars like Aranda and Alemán have done much to trouble the idea put forth in Sánchez and Pita's (1992) introduction to *The Squatter and the Don* that situates it as a subaltern text anticipating a future proletarian Chicana/o subject.

The complex hermeneutics of Ruiz de Burton scholarship redoubled with the recovery of her first novel, *Who Would Have Thought It?* (1995), three years after her second novel, *The Squatter and the Don*, had been republished. *Who Would Have Thought It?* further complicated Ruiz de Burton's initial recovery as a contestatory author because it places even more emphasis on the heroine's whiteness and is, in part, what sparked the reassessment of Ruiz de Burton's position in Chicana/o literary history. Set in New England during the Civil War, the Mexican American protagonist of *Who Would Have Thought It?*, Lola Medina, is surrounded and overshadowed by the New Englanders, who both rescue her and try to steal her inheritance. At the beginning of the story, Lola's skin is dyed black by Indian captors, and it slowly fades throughout the narrative. *Who Would Have Thought It?* performs its own critique of U.S. forms of time by recasting the celebrated newness of U.S. modernity as petty and provincial in comparison to global timescales of colonization and national development. Like *The Squatter and the Don*, it also mocks U.S. legal systems (especially bureaucracy) as backward and inefficient.

Though Sánchez and Pita recovered Ruiz de Burton's *Who Would Have Thought It?* in 1995 and her personal correspondence in 2001, *The Squatter and the Don*'s 1992 recovery structured academic conversations about the author, because it was the text through which scholars initially read her. There is an interesting error on the back cover of Arte Público's 1995 reprint of *Who Would Have Thought It?* that reads, "As in her first novel, *The Squatter and the Don* (1885), Ruiz de Burton reserves critical barbs for corruption in government and United States expansion. . . . However, it is in the recasting of the conventional novel of domesticity that *Who Would Have Thought It?* also addresses the disenfranchisement of women." Accidentally calling *The Squatter and the Don* Ruiz de Burton's first novel is an interesting mistake, but so too is the logical structure of "However" that takes the *Squatter and the Don* as the critical starting point for analysis of *Who Would Have Thought It?*[12] Even though scholars clearly recognize that *The Squatter and the Don*, published over a decade after *Who Would Have Thought It?*, could not have affected the first novel, our critical conversations are shaped by the novels' reverse recovery.

The heterogeneous forms of time in both of Ruiz de Burton's books are, in part, a function of their genre—the novel—which is actually an amalgamation of many genres. The dialogic form of the novel brings together diverse discourses that carry with them multiple generic conventions. Some of the more notable genres dialoguing in *The Squatter and the Don* are romance, domestic fiction, legalistic discourse, jeremiad, and the novel of manners. But the novel's recovery adds another genre to this list: historical romance. Sánchez and Pita describe the novel as a historical romance on the first page of their introduction. Vincent Pérez (2000, 33), John Morán González (2004, 153), and Anne Goldman (1999, 79), who each played a significant role in shaping scholarly conversations about the novel, also refer to it as a historical romance.[13] But *The Squatter and the Don*'s emphasis on "contemporary events" places it, in my opinion, outside the genre of historical romance, as does the brief eight-year gap between the year of the novel's romantic closure and its publication.

The Squatter and the Don invokes a particular cultural memory. Its nostalgia is in line with a number of texts by Mexican Americans in the late nineteenth and early twentieth centuries, particularly the autobiographical writing recovered by Genaro Padilla's *My History, Not Yours* (1993), which included Ruiz de Burton's close friend Mariano Vallejo. Vincent Pérez writes that in Ruiz de Burton's novel, "Nostalgia for an idealized and unobtainable past serves a fundamental oppositional function, certainly enacting an imaginative communion with the narrator's lost family and community but also articulating resistance to sociocultural oppression in the United States" (2000, 39–40). But nostalgia does not make the novel a historical romance. Characters in a historical romance are not nostalgic for the past precisely because they are *in* the past. Don Mariano's nostalgia is part of what makes him contemporary within the 1870s; his perspective invokes the perspective of many disenfranchised elite Californios in the latter half of the nineteenth century. *The Squatter and the Don*, instead, becomes a historical novel for its recoverers. Sánchez and Pita are the ones who interpellate today's readers in the novel through a process of recovery that seeks continuity between past and present to contest and repair the ideological, if not the material, violence of U.S. colonization (1992, 49).

Ruiz de Burton's novel is at times a narrative of resistance—in its narrative digressions lambasting Congress' political corruption and railroad capitalists' moral bankruptcy—but it is also, and more fundamentally, what Marissa López calls a "resistant narrative" (2011, 121). Its multiple and divergent forms of time disrupt the ideology of linear progress, which is consequently the very temporality that shapes contestation as dialectic resolution within modern paradigms of reparation, restitution, and historical revision. This form of time is perhaps "the monster who has not ceased to be victorious" that holds sway over *contemporary* readers of all periods in U.S. modernity's colonized time (Sánchez and Pita 1992, 49). *The Squatter and the Don* remains contemporary, as it moves across multiple forms of time, from the moment of its composition to the time of its recovery. For this reason the text performs what Chela Sandoval calls "differential consciousness," the ability to shift between different ideological constructions at will, which is a "survival skill developed under subordination" (2000, 30). While Ruiz de Burton's class status and self-identified whiteness placed her within the privileged elite, her gender and emergent ethnic classification left her in a dependent and subordinate position on a number of occasions. Perhaps it is the complexity of her life that gave her the skills to "juggle, transgress, differ, buy, and sell ideologies in a system of production and exchange bent on ensuring survival," traveling "with literacy across and through cultural spaces" (Sandoval 2000, 30). Though not a decolonial text, *The Squatter and the Don* displays a differential time consciousness in its shifting ideological deconstruction of U.S. modernity.

The Squatter and the Don's differential time consciousness calls for the discontinuation of linear, progressive time; neither social integration nor social uprising adequately addresses the temporal colonization of Californios because both possibilities perpetuate a linear, progressive time that acts through dialectic resolution. Textual recovery and the revision of literary history often rely on paradigms of national or biological origin, linear historical narratives, and assessments of cultural development that are all structured by an underlying reliance on linear homogenous time. *The Squatter and the Don's* recovery in the 1990s and 2000s was highly contested, as scholars participated in a conversation about how Ruiz de Burton and her book fit into Chicana/o literary history. Marissa López's question in *Chicano Nations*—"What constitutes a resistant narrative and how is it different from a narrative of resistance?"— sheds light on the process of recovery, particularly for *The Squatter and the Don* (2011, 121). The novel's contradictory content complicates its status as a narrative of resistance, but its contradictory forms of time makes it a resistant narrative—resistant as much to contemporary interpretation as it is to the nineteenth-century U.S. colonization of time.

CHAPTER 2

Progress in the Land of Poco Tiempo

Miguel Antonio Otero's Political Vision

In many ways Miguel Antonio Otero embodies the political and economic enfranchisement that the Alamars of *The Squatter and the Don* seek throughout María Amparo Ruiz de Burton's novel. Otero was a socialite and a politician. The son of an elite Nuevomexicano and a southern belle, Otero's father was successful in bringing the Atchison, Topeka and Santa Fe Railroad to New Mexico. Otero's family's business and political success rested on the kind of racial and power consolidation between elite Hispanos and Anglos that the Mechlins and Alamars are unable to enact in *The Squatter and the Don*. Through him we might imagine what Gabriel's and Lizzie's life could have been had the railroad arrived in San Diego. Otero worked as a banker in Las Vegas, New Mexico. His father had been a U.S. representative for the territory, and Otero began his own political career as the city clerk, county clerk, probate clerk, and then district court clerk. In 1896 President William McKinley appointed Otero governor of the territory in a surprise move after meeting him at the Republican National Convention in 1892. Otero garnered support within the territory as the first territorial governor who came from the territory, and he led a group of young up-start politicians who called themselves the Colts. Otero served as governor for nine years (1897–1906), and statehood became the primary focus of his political career. Late in life he published a three-volume autobiography, *My Life on the Frontier* (1935, 1939) and *My Nine Years as Governor* (1940), and a biography titled *The Real Billy the Kid: With New Light on the Lincoln County War* (1936 [1998]).

In his literary and political writing, Otero emphasized New Mexico's participation in U.S. modernity, and he presented himself as a key figure in modernizing the territory. Yet, like Ruiz de Burton, Otero became a critic of the U.S. federal government. As the first Nuevomexicano governor appointed to New Mexico territory, he was also the first governor to meaningfully address the political disenfranchisement that stemmed from more than sixty years of territorial status. Otero coupled the rhetoric of progress with a push for material modernization in an attempt to prove that New Mexico merited statehood. He likewise tried to distance the territory from regionalist writers' popular narratives that aestheticized Nuevomexicanos as slow-moving, ever-late remnants of an earlier time. The territory did not gain statehood during his tenure as governor, but Otero's writing reveals the disjuncture between forms of time concerned with sociological progress and forms of time concerned with technological progress, highlighting the way that U.S. politics moved between the two to exclude Mexican Americans from U.S. modernity.

The nation's spatiotemporal structure was undergoing change during Otero's political career, and this reconfiguration was important to his own constructions of time for New Mexico. The massive Western (spatial) expansion of the nineteenth century was coming to an end, and the U.S. practice of empire building was also undergoing change. Thomas M. Allen asserts that U.S. spatial expansion of the eighteenth and nineteenth centuries acted as a trope for U.S. expansion into the future, where the paradox of an imperialist democracy could be ideologically resolved by aligning the U.S. West with newness and regeneration. U.S. frontiersmen were thus not violently traveling across a populated space but moving "toward a utopian horizon in the future where the nation's contradictions would resolve themselves into a coherent republic" (2008, 23). The end of that spatial expansion—marked in part by Frederick Jackson Turner's 1893 claim that the frontier was closed— forced a reworking of tropes about U.S. progress. The United States needed to progress into the future through methods not so closely tied to spatial expansion. Ironically, modernist writing about the U.S. West, often in the form of regionalist writing, continued to aestheticize the land as a space of spiritual renewal and escape from the constraints of an industrialized and socially restrictive Northeast—through a journey not to the future but to the past. The writing and political activism of regionalist authors such as Mary Austin and Mabel Dodge Luhan ostensibly sought to preserve local practices in the face of modernization. Otero's political career began around the time that Turner declared the frontier closed, and he published his literary works after the Santa Fe and Taos writers colonies had been well established as centers of modernist writing. Otero's temporal politics pushed against both the modernist vein of regional writing and the nineteenth-century rhetoric of progress as territorial expansion to map a different kind of modernity onto the territory, one that centered on New Mexico's centrality to U.S. modernity.

Peter Osborne's articulation of modernity, modernization, and modernism as three distinct yet interrelated concepts with their own ideological under-pinnings is helpful here. *Modernity* is specifically and paradoxically an epoch of the present, the period of homogenous, empty, linear temporality through which it is defined. *Modernization*, in contrast, is a process of development with roots in European and Euro-American economic and cultural values. For Osborne modernization "provide[s] a content to fill the form of the modern, to give it something more than an abstract temporal determinacy" (1996, 17). Modernization creates a way of understanding time that is inter-twined with both the mechanisms of capitalism and the racialized invention of colonial difference. *Modernism* (practiced by modernists), in contrast, is the "affirmative cultural self-consciousness" of modernity as well as an "aes-theticization of modernity" (23, 12). Such aestheticization is present not only in the high modernist art of Europe and the Americas but also in popular culture and noncanonical or alternate representations of modernity. The plurality of modernisms highlights the durability and flexibility of modernity as a temporal structure. Otero's attempts to *modernize* New Mexico to meet Anglo-American social and economic demands never admitted him or New Mexico into the fold of U.S. *modernity* because *modernist* U.S. political and literary representations of New Mexico and Nuevomexicanos continued to place them outside the temporal flow of modern historical subjectivity.

Turner's Frontier Thesis had described the U.S. process of modernization historically by spatializing sociological progress as repetition. Anglo-Americans repeat the successive phases of social development as they move across the frontier, reverting to hunters and traders, then developing into farmers and ultimately industrialists as a "perennial rebirth" that "dominates the American character" (1993, 60). While the economic, political, and social trajectories of development could be repeated, the biologically prescribed trajectory of racial development could not. Having already reached the pinnacle of historical progress, only western Europeans were capable of repeating the cycle as a condensed process of cultural regeneration, and that regeneration consolidated whiteness, transforming European immigrants into Americans. Turner's evolutionary history of the United States conveniently ignores the Native Americans who continued to live in the nation's territory long past the frontier's movement west to the Pacific. It also omits Mexican Americans and the U.S.-Mexico War and subordinates the importance of the Civil War, with its own complex racial history, to the evolution of the U.S. western frontier. Turner deracinates U.S. history by casting Anglo-Americans not only as the epitome of social development but, in fact, as the only actors participating in any development at all.

With its destiny of stretching from the Atlantic to the Pacific seemingly manifest by the end of the nineteenth century, U.S. political focus shifted to incorporating western territories into the national body politic through industrialization and the political participation of statehood. This process of incorporation dovetailed with the Progressive Era's diverse social and political movements, which increased federal and state regulation by focusing on the systematic organization and bureaucratization of the government. In this way U.S. modernization was refigured as reform rather than expansion. The transition appeared as an opportunity to Otero. Long a champion of Progressive politics, Otero joined the Progressive Party in 1912. His position as a Nuevomexicano in conquered Mexican territory barred him from the ideology of progress as westward movement, and so Otero inserted himself into national development by reconfiguring what it meant to bring progress to the frontier. His autobiography begins with an account of his childhood travels westward on the Atchison, Topeka and Santa Fe Railroad. Otero performs a spatiotemporal sleight of hand by moving west in the opening pages of his autobiography, aligning himself with the movement of U.S. frontiersmen and the "progress" they bring although he is, in fact, returning to his family home in New Mexico. Yet his movement from east to west is not so much participation as it is a usurpation of the ideological power of civilizing the U.S. West. The wild element that Otero observes as he travels is predominantly composed of Anglo-American desperados.

Juan Bruce-Novoa asserts that through this opening move, "Otero wrote himself into the westward-expanding frontier by fusing his origin with the railroad, the epitome of nineteenth-century progress" and linked the foreign Spanish community of New Mexico to U.S. industrial centers by squeezing out the uncivilized space between them, the zone of Indian "wildness" that threatened both New Mexico territory and U.S. states (2003, 112, 115–16). But, while Otero was keenly aware of Anglo-Americans' prejudice against Spanish Americans, he never equated his ethnic identity with foreignness. Instead, he repeatedly referred to himself and other Nuevomexicanos as "native," a term that specifically contested the position of Mexican Americans as foreigners in their own land, to paraphrase San Antonio mayor Juan N. Seguín (2002). Like popular nativist movements of the period, Otero's terminology naturalizes the place of Nuevomexicanos' within the nation.[1] Importantly, rail travel played a key role in policing racial boundaries through its enforcement of segregation. Justice John Marshall Harlan made clear the extent of the railroads' symbolic power in his dissent to *Plessy vs. Ferguson*, when he argued, "'Personal liberty,' it has been well said, 'consists in the power of locomotion, of changing situation, or removing one's person to whatsoever places one's own inclination may direct, without imprisonment or restraint'" (1896). Here "locomotion" blurs the boundaries between spatial and temporal movement, while it highlights how the ability to change one's situation is racially determined. Otero's extensive railroad travels from an early age position him as a full (white) citizen and participant in U.S. national time.[2]

Otero's childhood observations show that, rather than joining a "foreign" New Mexico to the east, he subtly supplants the "civilizing" force of Anglo-American immigrants with native Nuevomexicano civility, reversing the polarity of U.S. progress. The Wild West is peopled with Anglo outlaws and unstable boomtowns in contrast to Otero's family members in New Mexico, who embody efficient and honest business practices. Picaresque childhood encounters with Anglo Wild Westerners in the first volume of his autobiography become a proleptic metaphor for the third volume, where Governor Otero is a force of progress who combats economic and political corruption. As an overdetermined symbol of modernity, the railroad does a great deal of work in situating the Oteros as the territory's modernizers. Miguel Otero emphasizes his father's role in bringing the Atchison, Topeka and Santa Fe to the territory to position his family as the modernizing force in New Mexico. The arrival of the rail line brings New Mexico into the folds of U.S. standard time, which the railroads invented and installed throughout the nation.

Rewriting the Western

Otero positions himself and his family as the harbingers of modernization in New Mexico, contra a markedly uncivilized U.S. Wild West. In each volume of his autobiography, Otero develops and refines an assertion that he and his family are the modernizers of New Mexico who brought technological and economic advancement in the form of railroads, telephone service, and financial institutions. He likewise presents himself as the territory's champion during its struggle to enter U.S. modernity as a politically enfranchised state. Drawing on popular U.S. tropes, Otero positions New Mexicans as modernizing frontiersmen, with himself as their western hero.

The first volume of the autobiography is a picaresque narrative of Otero's adventures growing up in the Wild West, where he meets famous figures such as Buffalo Bill, Calamity Jane, and Billy the Kid. These adventures set the stage for Otero's political ascendancy in the later two volumes. It is precisely the depoliticized naïveté of childhood in Otero's first autobiography that permits his reversal of U.S. racialized narratives of sociopolitical development. In volume 1 Otero eulogizes the passing of the old West in the same way that nineteenth-century Anglo authors eulogized the disappearance of Native Americans. Like Ruiz de Burton's novels, Otero's writing works in conversation with U.S. imperialist nostalgia, but instead of refuting the trope, Otero repurposes it. Richard Slotkin (1973) describes a unique permutation of imperialist nostalgia in the myth of the U.S. West, calling it a process of "regeneration through violence." In Slotkin's formulation Indians first teach an archetypal Anglo-American how to survive in the wilderness of the U.S. frontier and then, as Renato Rosaldo summarizes, "the disciple turns on his spiritual masters and achieves redemption by killing them" (1993, 72). But Otero draws on the myth of the U.S. West and the trope of imperialist nostalgia, not to eulogize the passing of New Mexico's Spanish heritage, like regional modernists, or the disappearance of Native Americans, like authors of Anglo-American westerns, but to reminisce about the modernization of a distinctly Anglo Wild West. His "spiritual masters" are not the Indians of Slotkin's analysis but the Anglo westerners and frontiersmen who had sup-planted natives in the original U.S. imperialist discourse.

By crediting Anglo-Americans for much of his moral and cultural formation, Otero has become a problematic figure for Chicana/o history and literary recovery that seek narratives of contestation and political resistance. Yet it is the form rather than the content of his autobiography that belies a differential time consciousness through its subtle reversal of spatial and racial tropes of development. The Wild Westerners in Otero's autobiographical history act as simulacra for the "original" frontier, which Otero conquers metonymically through his political campaign of modernization and reform. Otero subsumes the rugged individualistic identities of the Wild West figures he encounters, incorporating their characteristics into his own powerful political persona. "I found myself thrown altogether upon my own resources," Otero writes on the last page of *My Life on the Frontier*, volume 1, "but I soon learned that in this life one must depend largely on oneself, and I was not long in learning my lesson, for I had gained a wonderful experience for one so young by my association with men who were much older than myself, and I meant to use the knowledge thus acquired judiciously, fearlessly and honestly" (1935, 288). Even as he acknowledges the old westerners of his childhood travels, Otero erases them. Their resources become his resources; their knowledge becomes his self-reliance. Otero envisions himself as supplanting not a natural wilder-ness but the wildness of an Anglo-American old West through political and economic modernization.

Otero's narrative strategy in the multivolume autobiography is more than a repurposing of literary tropes. The forms of time in the autobiographical account change in accordance with Otero's rise to power and the corresponding order and organization that he supposedly brings to New Mexico. The entire first volume is a series of adventuresome, picaresque vignettes that focus on Otero's youth. Consequently, the narrative's explanatory power is cumulative rather than linear. By the end of the book, Otero's gain in consciousness appears to be ex nihilo because the cause and effect of his maturation is obscured by the narrative form. It is difficult to discern the chronological order of events in volume 1. For example, a gambling incident involving Otero's political nemesis, Thomas Catron, occurs sometime between 1866 (when La Fonda of Las Vegas is founded) and 1880 (the historical point in the narrative from which Otero is recounting the events), but this time frame encompasses almost the entire volume, which covers 1864 to 1882. In contrast, *My Nine Years as Governor* is clearly sequential and rarely disrupted by digressive reminiscence. The clarity and organization of this final volume parallel Otero's "businesslike admin-istration," and the book draws distinct causal relationships between Otero's actions and the positive results they produce (1935, 286). Though both the first and the third volume are ostensibly about the historical development of New Mexico, their varying structures give them different explanatory power. While the deployment of tropes from the "myth of the West" in volume 1 naturalizes an Anglo-American past, it also naturalizes Anglo-Americans *as* past. To an extent this process performs what Roland Barthes calls "the best weapon against myth," which is "to mythify it in its turn" (2012, 135).

But while Otero's writing undermines one form of time in the narrative of Anglo-American progress, it continues to promote linear, progressive time as the sole temporality for achieving self-determination. This is apparent in both the structure and the content of *My Nine Years as Governor*. John-Michael Rivera explains that Otero's biography of the famous New Mexico outlaw, *The Real Billy the Kid*, "renders Nuevomexicano bourgeois men [rather than Anglos . . .] as the direct civilizers of the 'new' New Mexico at the turn of the century" (2000, 55). The autobiographies do likewise, but the replacement of bourgeois Anglo-American men by bourgeois Nuevomexicanos does little to critique the underlying temporal structure of U.S. modernity. Unlike *The Squatter and the Don*, Otero's writing does not deconstruct U.S. modernity's temporal economy. Instead, his work enacts a permutation of what Chela

Sandoval calls metaideologizing. Like Barthes's tactic of mythifying the myth, metaideologizing is "the operation of appropriating dominant ideological forms, and using them whole in order to transform them" (2000, 83). Like Ruiz de Burton, Otero's differential consciousness is partial and highly compromised by his own stake in the hegemony of settler colonialism. While it is a far cry from Chicana feminists' remaking of the Malinche figure, Otero nonetheless demonstrates semiological adroitness in his repurposing of the myth of the U.S. West.

Volume 2 of *My Life on the Frontier* is a transitional narrative, in both style and content, between Otero's carefree, disorganized, youthful memories and his official and orderly record as governor. Otero becomes involved in local politics, where he is more thoroughly acquainted with the corruption of New Mexico politicians, particularly a cohort known as the Santa Fe Ring. In one chapter of this volume, Otero depicts his own battle over land rights with the Santa Fe Ring in a form reminiscent of the Wild West showdown between Billy the Kid and the Dolan-Murphy clan during the Lincoln County War.[3] In the 1870s the Santa Fe Ring manipulated a land grant to obtain the Nuestra Señora de los Dolores mine, which belonged to the Otero family. Because the ring controlled both the surveyor and the territory's chief justice, the Oteros were unable to reclaim the mine legally, and so Miguel Otero decided to give up the court battle and take the mine by force. Otero and his cohorts captured the mine, renaming their holding Fort Otero. The presiding judge throughout Otero's court battle was none other than Samuel B. Axtell, the former territorial governor whose ineptitude had helped inflame the Lincoln County War. With characteristic gusto Otero asserts, "Axtell's initials [S.B.] seemed at least very appropriate, and surely they were" (1939, 87).

What is even more appropriate is Otero's triumph over Axtell and the ring where Billy the Kid had failed in the Lincoln County War. Initially, Otero is summoned to court and held in contempt. He arrives in court, not because he is captured by the ring but because he feels obligated to return to Las Vegas when the San Miguel National Bank needs him to fill out paperwork, and thus he surrenders to the sheriff to fulfill his duties at the bank. In the end Otero achieves success through the legal system when he is acquitted by a grand jury. President Grover Cleveland subsequently removes Judge Axtell, and the courts decide the mine case in Otero's favor. This incident is one of the most complexly constructed accounts in the autobiography, particularly in light of the fact that Otero's was a pyrrhic victory. Like many Nuevomexicanos, Otero was "double crossed" by his own lawyers, who received portions of the mine as payment and then manipulated the land grant such that Otero lost almost $20,000 in the venture (Otero 1939, 89). Otero glosses over this outcome in a single paragraph, however, because it is imperative to Otero's narrative that he remain triumphant to fulfill his literary role as New Mexico's modernizing harbinger of progress. Otero "wins" the dispute over his mine not by force but through the legal system after he demonstrates his full integration into the efficient administration of capitalism as a bank teller. Like Clarence Darrell in the *Squatter and the Don*, Otero uses modernity's empty homogenous time to his own ends. He depicts modernity's future-focused, linear progress as a process of reform rather than expansion, but Otero's ability to control time is purely narrative, not material in the way that Darrell's stock trading is, and thus he loses rather than gains capital.

By the time Otero appears in *My Nine Years as Governor*, his Wild West showdowns are purely political. In 1903 Otero performs the role of western hero to perfection in a heated argument with President Theodore Roosevelt when he realizes that the president is opposing New Mexico statehood. In this scene President Roosevelt embodies the kind of pomp and grandeur that Otero had condemned in a childhood encounter with Buffalo Bill. In fact, Buffalo Bill had helped spread the fame of Roosevelt and his Rough Riders in the 1898 show *Buffalo Bill's Wild West and Congress of Rough Riders of the World*, and Buffalo Bill's self-aggrandizement in volume 1 of Otero's autobiography is in many ways a prefiguration of Roosevelt's personality in the third volume.[4] During the political confrontation Roosevelt tells Otero, "If I were in your place, I would remain a territory as long as the United States government will pay your running expenses," adding that, with New Mexico as a territory, its corrupt judges could be removed by the executive branch. Otero explains, "Mr. Roosevelt became very much excited when I did not agree with him, and in most eloquent words tried to impress me that all judges in the West were corrupt. He wound up his spleen by saying: 'Governor Otero, I think a corrupt judge ought to be taken out to the corral, tied to a cow's tail, and sh— to death.' I smilingly agreed to his sentiment, but insisted that we had many honest and capable judges in New Mexico, much better than those sent out to us by politicians in the East" (1940, 216). Roosevelt tries to convince Otero that the narrative of New Mexican underdevelopment and political unfitness originated in the West and in the racialized Nuevomexicanos who lived there, but Otero reverses the directionality of mismanagement and credits Washington with appointing corrupt judges in the territory. Otero later explains that Roosevelt "never outgrew the selfishness and self-display characteristic of children" (315), and the childish president consequently made "several removals [of local politicians] in New Mexico that [Otero] considered arbitrary and unjust" (326).

Otero's rivalry with Roosevelt is interesting because the president was perhaps the most prominent figure of Progressive Era politics, and like Roosevelt, Otero would later join the Progressive Party. Otero's conflict with the president and his other critiques of U.S. government trouble scholarly readings of him as an "Americanized," assimilationist Nuevomexicano. Otero's writing is much more complex than these readings would suggest. Like Ruiz de Burton's recovery as a contestatory author, the simplification of Otero as noncontestatory places him on one *side* of U.S. history—the side of acculturation and U.S. domination. Ironically, reading Otero as an assimilationist denies his presence within Chicana/o literary history in the same way that U.S. temporal colonization denied Nuevomexicano presence within narratives of sociological development. Bruce-Novoa (2005) aptly explains that "although some Chicano critics would rather not acknowledge [Otero] on grounds of his class and privilege, these may be exactly the reasons for giving him the attention he merits if nothing else for the quality of his writing." Indeed, their privileged access to print culture and the ability to control time—not only narrative time but also the actual, substantial, time they were able to allocate to writing books—makes authors like Otero and Ruiz de Burton the most recoverable, if not the most palatable. Despite Bruce-Novoa's and Rivera's efforts to recover Otero's writing, the Nuevomexicano governor is not studied nearly as much as authors whose work was initially recovered as explicitly contestatory. Otero's persistent belief in progress never granted him or New Mexico full access to *presence* within U.S. modernity and its political processes. Ironically, his emphasis on New Mexico progress and U.S. structures of modernization has impeded his presence within literary recovery that privileged a contestation paradigm for Mexican American authors.

The Art of Disenfranchisement

Progressive Era politics gave Otero a platform for espousing the rhetoric of reform as a means of progress for New Mexico and the United States. In his first speech to New Mexicans as governor, Otero promised his "earnest effort to have a sound, honest, and firm business administration," signaling his goal to modernize the territory through reform of its corrupt political machine (1939, 300). But the Progressive Era's reform marked a refiguration of U.S. modernity's colonial temporality rather than a transformation of its oppressive and racist uses of time. Progressive Era reform was in many ways a repetition (with a difference) of the United States' mid-nineteenth-century colonization of time. It marked a consolidation of power through the systemization and bureaucratization of government purported to help end corruption. The power of the executive branch increased dramatically under Theodore Roosevelt, who exercised his ability to regulate corporations and reserve federal land more than any previous president. At the same time U.S. capitalism witnessed a consolidation of economic power. Lewis L. Gould explains, "For the seven years after 1897, more than 4,200 companies in the United States turned into 257 corporations" (2001, 25). While industrial workers benefited from some of the period's social reform that restricted work hours, regulated child labor, and improved sanitation and food safety, many Progressive politicians, especially Roosevelt, were "conservative . . . at heart" and "wanted to provide gradual change to stave off more sweeping alterations in the nation's order" (35).

Indeed, while the Progressive Era was a period of major social reform for working-class Anglo men and women, it marked an intensification of racial oppression for many Americans. The 1890s saw the rise of the Immigration Restriction League and the Supreme Court approval of segregation, which legitimated Jim Crow laws. "There was a degree of social control and political coercion behind some of the progressive rhetoric," Gould writes; "For many white Southerners, the development of segregation in the 1890s went forward as a 'reform' of the existing structure of race relations" (2001, 13). Thus, the era's consolidation of power also signaled a new institutionalization of racial hierarchies. For racialized subjects in the United States, Progressive Era politics typified modernity as "ever new, but always, in its newness, the same" (Osborne 1996, 13).

Otero's racial politics relied on allying elite Nuevomexicanos with incoming Anglo-Americans. His literary representations of African Americans and Native Americans align him with the institutionalization of racism by Progressive politics, though his rhetoric of reform generally elided racial difference within the New Mexico body politic for the sake of gaining political sovereignty through statehood. Like Roosevelt, Otero sought to expand his executive power in New Mexico. For example, he asked the Thirty-Sixth New Mexico Legislative Assembly to create new offices under his direction, such as those of the insurance commissioner and irrigation engineer. He also sought the authority "to remove summarily county officials accepting illegal fees, or county commissions accepting such illegal fees. Also of county officials guilty of nonfeasance, misfeasance, or malfeasance in office [*sic*]" (1940, 368). These regulations and many others were part of Otero's effort to defeat powerful political machines in the territory, which were both his primary political opposition and a hindrance to the territory's statehood prospects.[5] Otero reworks progress as *reform* rather than *expansion* in his political writing and his speeches to delink New Mexico's geographic position from its temporal position with the United States' historical narrative of development. His insistence on New Mexico's progress—its movement through time—much like Ruiz de Burton's insistence on Californio presence, works to insert the territory into U.S. modernity.

The U.S. colonization of New Mexico's time, like the colonization of Californio time depicted in *The Squatter and the Don*, drew on a conjunction of economic and political disenfranchisement. New Mexico had been seeking statehood for almost half a century by the time Otero was appointed governor in 1897. The Treaty of Guadalupe Hidalgo's promise to admit conquered Mexican territory into the United States "at the proper time" was the most egregiously delayed for New Mexico. Almost fifty statehood bills were sent to Congress between 1850 and 1897, and each of them was rejected. Citizens in the territory were not allowed to vote for their governor or for the president, and decisions made by the elected territorial legislature were subject to federal approval. While former Mexicans and their descendants awaited the "proper time" to be admitted to the enjoyment of full citizen rights, the "mean time" placed Nuevomexicanos in a liminal phase of territoriality. As with Californios, the U.S. government did not protect the liberty and property of Nuevomexicanos but, rather, initiated policies that dispossessed former Mexicans of land and excluded them from democratic participation. New Mexico had been established as a territory during the 1850 compromise that admitted California as a state; as Richard Griswold del Castillo explains, "Because New Mexico became a territory rather than a state, the civil rights were less than those in California" (1990, 70). New Mexico demonstrates, perhaps better than any other territory, what the "mean time" really looked like for Mexican Americans awaiting full political enfranchisement—the installation of long-term colonial dependency and economic underdevelopment. Otero's attempt to recast New Mexico through the modernizing process of reform rather than expansion was both rhetorical and material. His political career coupled an anticorruption, proefficiency economic development platform, with depictions of New Mexico at the forefront of civility, self-sufficiency, and economic growth, all with the intent of attaining statehood.

In the mean time, between U.S. conquest and statehood, Anglo-American politicians and writers cast New Mexico's underdevelopment as a trait of its native population rather than the design of U.S. colonization. In 1893 Charles Lummis described the region as the land of *poco tiempo* in his book of that title (1913). His first chapter artistically mirrors political justifications for not admitting the territory to statehood. He depicts New Mexico as the "National Rip Van Winkle—the United States which is *not* United States. Here is the land of *poco tiempo*—the home of 'Pretty Soon.' Why hurry with the hurrying world? The 'Pretty Soon' of New Spain is better than the 'Now! Now!' of the haggard States. The opiate sun soothes to rest, the adobe is made to lean against, the hush of day-long noon would not be broken. Let us not hasten— *mañana* will do. Better still, *pasado mañana*" (1913, 3). As Genaro Padilla writes, "Lummis authorized and instituted a language that has reverberated in other travel narratives, magazine articles, scholarly studies, poetry, novels, and theater of the region down to the present" (1993, 208).

Lummis's *Land of Poco Tiempo*, like the Treaty of Guadalupe Hidalgo's mean time, works to deny New Mexico admission to the temporal flow of modernity within the United States. Directly translated as "little time," the *poco tiempo* that Lummis assigns the territory is actually a lack or absence of time. Lummis and his cohort were extolled as part of a liberal project to promote the region through art and historical preservation. But as John Nieto-Phillips observes, "These artists and intellectuals who retreated to the Southwest to escape the dehumanizing effects of an alienating industrial and urban society on the East Coast often participated in the dehumanization of their subjects, or better put, their objects—Mexicans and Native Americans" (2004, 210). That dehumanization was enacted in part by aestheticizing Nuevomexicanos and Native peoples as objects outside the flow of modernity. *The Land of Poco Tiempo* describes "New Spain," not the U.S. territory of New Mexico; the land itself and the warm, centuries-old adobe metonymically depict a culture of procrastination. But Lummis's *mañana* is a more apt assessment of the United States' repeated deferral of Nuevomexicano enfranchisement.

Even later artists and authors who championed cultural pluralism in the Southwest and promoted indigenous and Nuevomexicano cultural production tended to objectify the local population. Mary Austin's short piece "Why I Live in Santa Fe," published in 1932, long after Otero had retired and New Mexico had attained statehood, says of the state capital: "Here I find three things which my experience has led me to select as most desirable; it is a mountain country . . . , it is contiguous to the desert with its appeal of mystery and naked space, and it supplies the element of aboriginal society, which I have learned to recognize as my proper medium." Native Americans are here presented as a "medium," much like oil paints or pastels, not as co-producers of art. Austin goes on to describe "the next most intriguing group, the half way between, which is supplied by the Spanish-speaking population of New Mexico, the range and quality of which goes by the name of folk culture." She concludes that other southwestern locations offer access to these ethic groups, which are "the basis of all the wisdom I have. . . . But there are none which offer also the third range of complete intellectual sophistication as does Santa Fe." The city hosts "the first rank of creative and intellectual peo-ple" (306), whom Austin goes on to list in an exclusively Anglo-American selection of authors, scientists, anthropologists, and social reformers. Austin reproduces the sociological hierarchy of "aboriginal society," followed by "half way between" Nuevomexicanos and culminating in Anglo-American civilization and intellect. She prefers Santa Fe because it brings together her (dehumanized) artistic "medium"—Natives and Nuevomexicanos—and her intellectual peers, Anglos.

Indeed, the artistic promotion of New Mexico was by no means an economic or political promotion of the territory. Politicians working to disenfranchise Nuevomexicanos played on the very same stereotypes of stasis, inefficiency, and underdevelopment that literary authors used to champion the region as an escapist haven for artists. In a 1902 report to the Senate, Senator Beveridge of Indiana claimed that the available irrigation would take at least a generation of research before it could "support . . . successful agriculture" and that the majority of New Mexicans lived in "mud houses."[6] While Lummis's sunbaked adobe is more picturesque than Beveridge's mud houses, both men fuse images of landscape and people that are equally outside of U.S. modernity. Even President McKinley, who had shown apparent faith in New Mexico self-governance by appointing a Nuevomexicano governor, saw a similar parallel between land and humans. Visiting New Mexico in 1901, he told residents that they would need "more water and people" before the territory could become a state (qtd. in Holtby 2012, 72). "People," in this sense, is a gloss for Anglo-American people. Like Mary Austin's depiction of both land and natives as her artistic medium, McKinley dehumanizes Native Americans and Nuevomexicanos and subtly aligns them with the unproductive desert land.

The number of people in New Mexico was important. Statehood was directed by the Northwest Ordinance of 1787, originally designed to incorporate territory just west of the Appalachian Mountains and south of the Great Lakes. It allowed for the election of a nonvoting delegate to Congress once the population had reached "five thousand free male inhabitants of full age." Otero's father had served as New Mexico's territorial delegate from 1856 to 1861. Territories had the opportunity to elect statehood once the population reached sixty thousand. The Northwest Ordinance imagined an unpopulated West, an empty space into which Anglo-Americans would move (though, much like the Treaty of Guadalupe Hidalgo, it claimed that "the utmost good faith shall always be observed toward the Indians"). New Mexico, however, disrupted that spatial imaginary because it already had more than sixty thousand free male inhabitants when the Treaty of Guadalupe Hidalgo assigned white U.S. citizenship to former Mexicans. Thus, New Mexico did not actually need more people to become a state; it needed a population racially commensurate with the desires of Congress. During much of his governorship, Otero focused on appeasing Washington politicians by promoting Anglo-American immigration and investment in the territory and presenting images of New Mexicans as socially, economically, and technologically modernized. But his later political speeches and writing openly attributes New Mexico's underdevelopment to Anglo-American political and social structures that actively undermined Nuevomexicano civilization and progress.

Perhaps the best place to trace Otero's growing disillusionment with the federal government is in his lengthy and detailed governor's reports to the secretary of the interior (1901, 1902). Otero's reports were the longest governor's reports written in New Mexico from the time it became a territory until many years after Otero's governorship. According to Otero, the government printing office once told him that one of his reports was the best governor's report ever submitted (1940, 199). Each year Otero included a section in the report, which he personally wrote, outlining the reasons New Mexico deserved statehood. After 1899 he also included a copy of the "state" constitution, written and adopted by the Constitutional Convention held at Santa Fe in 1889. In his 1901 report Otero described New Mexico's constitution as "the best ever formulated in the United States," leaving it to readers' imagination to determine if he was including the national constitution in that assessment (26). Otero's call for statehood in the governor's reports grew more adamant throughout his time in office. His first report included a small section titled "Statehood," which was barely half of a page in length. By 1900, however, his statehood section was almost twenty pages long and included harsh language urging statehood. In 1902 Otero wrote a list of reasons why New Mexico "demand[ed]" statehood, invoking phrases reminiscent of colonial America. He argued that New Mexico was experiencing taxation without representation and wrote, "To hold [New Mexico citizens] longer in the Territorial vassalage will be a crime against American institutions" (21).

Otero asserted that any underdevelopment in the territory was a product of Anglo-American and not Nuevomexicano governance. The federal government's paternalistic role of appointing governors to the territory had created rampant corruption and massive land grabs in the second half of the nineteenth century. New Mexico appointments were a means to personal, political, and economic gain for most appointees, and the federal government paid little attention to how an appointee would affect the territory. For example, when Samuel B. Axtell was governor of Utah, residents accused him of being too pro-Mormon, so he asked President Ulysses S. Grant to appoint him as governor of New Mexico instead. Grant's responding telegram read, "Offer Axtell Governorship of New Mexico and appoint Emery in his place if he accepts. Emery may be appointed to New Mexico otherwise" (qtd. in Horn 1963, 175). For Grant and his appointees, territorial governors were interchangeable, not meant to represent a territory to the federal government but to represent the federal government within a territory. This kind of representation aligned the directionality of political influence with Turner's map of social progress, always moving from east to west.

Like Axtell, most New Mexico governors were not residents of the territory. Their appointments rested on the assumption that progress would have to come from outside of New Mexico, since Washington viewed the territory and its native population as fundamentally premodern. In reality, nonresident appointees had little interest in aiding the people of New Mexico. Another example of the inept federal appointees that New Mexico suffered before Otero took office is Robert Mitchell. Governor from 1866 to 1869, Mitchell traveled across New Mexico inspecting mining opportunities shortly after his appointment and then spent months in Washington DC, where, according to the *New Mexican*, he was trying to "sell stock in bogus gold mines" (qtd. in Horn 1963, 120). During Mitchell's absence, the secretary of the territory acted in his stead. When Mitchell returned he overturned all laws passed and all appointments filled by the secretary of the territory and the territorial legislature, but many appointed officials refused to step down for Mitchell's replacements. This period of chaos was one of many moments where poor federal governance impeded the territory's ability to function. While New Mexicans were accused of being backward and beyond the reach of modernity's temporal progression in popular and political rhetoric, the U.S. system of territorial dependency disrupted the region's economy and resulted in the kind of underdevelopment that politicians used as "evidence" of Nuevomexicanos' unfitness for self-governance. Thus, the mean time between U.S. colonization and statehood was not merely a period of waiting but rather a time of unsettling and reversing political processes through colonial oppression.

By the 1890s political rings had formed within the territory to fill the void in executive leadership, control local politics, and divide the spoils of U.S. land acquisition. Thomas Benton Catron led the Santa Fe Ring, which dominated the territory for over a decade. According to the *Silver City Enterprise*, Catron was one of the largest land-grant holders in the nation (cited in Larson 1968, 143). Unlike California, New Mexico's status as a territory meant that land claims were decided by the federal Office of the Surveyor General, significantly slower than California's state judiciary system (Griswold del Castillo 1990, 77). This office, like the territory's governor position, was subject to the caprices of Washington politics. Griswold del Castillo writes, "In 1885 the newly elected Democratic president, Grover Cleveland, removed the Republican surveyor general of New Mexico and replaced him with his own man, William Andrew Sparks, . . . [who was] 'steeped in prejudice against New Mexico, its people and their property rights'" (78–79).

Amid such instability, eastern transplant, lawyer, and politician Thomas Catron built an empire of several million acres on New Mexico land. Like other members of the Santa Fe Ring, Catron amassed much of his wealth by falsifying land-survey records to enlarge his holdings and by accepting land as payment for legal fees and defaulted loans. Though both Otero and Catron were members of the Republican Party, Otero positions Catron as his primary antagonist throughout *My Life on the Frontier* (vols. 1 and 2) and *My Nine Years as Governor*. Otero belittles him in all three volumes of his autobiography, often concluding anecdotes about Catron with the claim that all his schemes had come to naught. Though Otero's depictions reduce Catron's extensive political and economic power in the territory to a mere nuisance for the governor, he frames that nuisance in terms of repeatedly wasting time. Otero writes, "His attacks were so continuous and unyielding that I was compelled to make several unnecessary trips to Washington, at great expense, to explain his trumped up charges" (1940, 81). The expense is both financial and temporal—Catron disrupts capitalist efficiency and political progress. Otero's critique, while censuring the local and federal politics of Anglo-American domination, nonetheless remains heavily invested in the underlying concept of modern time and the power of modernization.

Elevating New Mexico in the Diachronic Scales of Development

Otero's focus on efficiency in government was part of his Progressive platform. His movement to combat waste, including wasted time, parallels another temporal move of his work—it distances itself from nostalgia for New Mexico's Spanish past. Just as Otero wanted to stop delays caused by wasted time, his investment in progress and modernization involved a turn away from the past as a locus of meaning and continuity. Other Nuevomexicano authors of the late nineteenth and early twentieth centuries utilized the popularity of Southwestern regionalism to contest Anglo domination through double-voiced narratives that longed for a pre-U.S. past. In contrast, Otero's autobiography and political actions place little emphasis on preserving or recording Nuevomexicano culture and folk practice, nor do they parallel the multigeneric, nonlinear structures that characterize many other Nuevomexicana/o autobiographies. For this reason, it is difficult to group Otero with proto-Chicana/o authors like Rafael and Eusebio Chacón, Nina Otero Warren, Fabiola Cabeza de Baca, or Josefina Niggli, who capitalized on and altered the kind of antimodern aesthetic that had drawn modernist authors like D. H. Lawrence and Mary Austin to the region. Nuevomexicana authors, in particular, tended to produce a "sentimental recall of the past . . . which question[ed] present authority" and critiqued "the Anglo's misunderstanding of Hispanic culture," as Tey Diana Rebolledo has argued (1990, 136; 1995, xxi). Their texts are grounded in the narrative of land loss. In contrast, Otero's depiction of the past repeatedly downplays the trauma of U.S. colonization and produces an individualistic (one might even say egotistical) narrative voice throughout his autobiography that aligns personal development with territorial progress.

Otero's intense push to position the territory within the present through the rhetoric of modernization and progress and his resistance to nostalgia that placed Nuevomexicanos in the past led him to denigrate New Mexico's cultural history. In a speech to Arizona residents, he said,

In New Mexico each year we have thousands of Eastern tourists who stop by for a day or two and delude themselves with the idea that they are making a study of the people and existing conditions. Few of them learn anything of value about the people or conditions as they actually exist. They are attracted by that which is novel and abnormal. They press the button upon every burro they meet. They are delighted to catch the features of a worthless old Indian. They photograph the oldest adobe building erected hundreds of years ago, and they return to their homes fully convinced and satisfied in their own minds that they know all about New Mexico, and that we are unfitted for statehood. (1940, 392–93)

This representation, along with some of Otero's political decisions (for example, his promotion of English-only education), has caused some scholars to identify Otero as "agringado" (Vigil 1980, 45) or, as Padilla describes him, a "culturally self-denying 'Spanish-American' territorial governor" (1993, 35). Yet Otero's antinostalgic representation shares with other Nuevomexicana/o authors the underlying intent of contesting the disenfranchisement of Mexican Americans by external U.S. forces. The difference is that his focus is decidedly on the present moment, to the detriment of New Mexico's past.

Otero's textual treatment of Native American communities is also indicative of his political focus on U.S. modernity. He denigrates Indians throughout his writing except when the mestizo heritage of Nuevomexicanos is cast as a reason to exclude them from self-governance. Otero revels in Indian killing in *The Real Billy the Kid*, writing, "The kid fell on them with his axe. In three minutes there was not a live Indian in sight but eight 'good Injuns' slept their last sleep" (1936 [1998], 18), and though he laments the killing of buffalo in his autobiography, Otero claims, "It had to be done to put an end to Indian depredations" (1935, x). Yet in a rare moment he claims mestizo heritage to defend Nuevomexicano fitness for self-government (though his grandparents were actually Spanish and Anglo-American). Otero's hastily written first governor's report had erroneously included a report by Indian agent Capt. Charles E. Nordstrom that referred to residents living outside the Zia pueblo as "greasers" unfit to serve on a jury. In response, Otero blotted out the report in every printed volume he could find and wrote an open letter to citizens of New Mexico that read, "I am a native Mexican myself and am proud of the fact. . . . I could never be guilty of the crime of casting any stain or reflection on my own or my father's ancestry, or the race to which we belong" (n.d., 2–3). No other evidence suggest that Otero identified as Mexican or mestizo at any other time, but Nordstrom's claim that a group of New Mexicans were unworthy to act as citizen jurors led Otero to defend and identify racially with mestizo Nuevomexicanos. Just as he had resignified the myth of the West, he resignifies racial and national heritage to place Nuevomexicanos in the fold of U.S. modernity. However, most of Otero's political writing deracinates New Mexico, making no distinction between Nuevomexicanos and Anglos, and focuses instead on political alliances to delink New Mexico from the sociological past to which it was relegated.

Otero's emphasis on modernity and the modernization of New Mexico was a temporal strategy to ascribe political and economic agency to Nuevo-mexicanos. Popular images of New Mexico's romantic past fed into a larger sociological discourse that organized peoples along a racial continuum of development. The modernist interest in the aesthetics of indigenous art and culture in New Mexico was part of a collusion among anthropologists, artists, the Bureau of Immigration, and the tourist industry that would later produce an embellished or invented Spanish colonial culture to promote the region. While Anglo and Nuevomexicano authors of the early twentieth century capitalized on regionalist modernism's fascination with Spanish colonial heritage, the logic of that fascination was built on ethnographic discourse. Ethnographic discourse denies "coevalness," as Johannes Fabian (2002) explains, depicting the cultural "other" observed by anthropologists (or, in this case, tourists) as habitants of a static time fundamentally different from the observer's experience of time as a progression through history. Nieto-Phillips details how the invention of New Mexico's tripartite culture reflects the denial of coevalness: "Only in New Mexico, boasted the bureau [of Immigration], could tourists witness the confluence of three distinct living peoples who exemplified three historical epochs and strata of civilizations: Pueblo Indians personified the earliest epoch and lowest stratum, Nuevomexicanos the middle, and Anglo Americans the superior" (2004, 128–29).

Regional authors like Mary Austin and Mabel Dodge Luhan sought to preserve the premodern, static essence they saw in New Mexico culture as a primitivist alternative to U.S. modernity. Thus, while their modernist writing critiques modernization, it nonetheless draws on modernity's timescale to situate New Mexico in an ahistorical, static past. For this reason Otero does not draw on romanticized Southwest folklore and local color in his political promotion of the territory or his later autobiographical writing. His temporal politics strove to insert New Mexico into the modern time of both U.S. democratic processes and capitalist accumulation. For Otero "progress" was a means to attaining presence—political and economic—within U.S. power structures.

On the few occasions that Otero does describe New Mexico's Spanish past, he reframes it through tropes of U.S. historical progress and modernization. In 1904 Otero gave a speech doing just that on New Mexico Day at the Louisiana Purchase Exposition, also known as the Saint Louis World's Fair. If the Chicago World's Fair: Columbian Exhibition, where Frederick Jackson Turner presented his Frontier Thesis, had been about U.S. exceptionalism and the triumph of progress and technology, then the Louisiana Purchase Exposition was about U.S. empire and global expansion. It presented a centennial celebration of the Louisiana Purchase but also featured a major exhibit of the nation's newest territorial acquisition from the Spanish-American War, the Philippines. Otero's speech worked to emphasize New Mexico's connection with the former and distance from the latter to argue, again, for statehood.

While the Santa Fe Trail seems the most obvious link between New Mexico and Missouri, Otero opens his speech by connecting the two regions through shared Spanish heritage: "The first land in the Louisiana Purchase was discovered by Spaniards, and their law rather than the French prevails in Louisiana and New Mexico" (1904, 3). At the same time he situates New Mexico as superior to the rest of the United States by saying, "The first settlement in the Louisiana Purchase was at Biloxi, Louisiana in 1699, when Santa Fe and other towns in New Mexico had been established for more than a hundred years under the civil or Roman law, which to a large extent prevails today in

New Mexico and Louisiana" (3, 2). In this way he remaps New Mexico as the center of North American law and civilization. Only after the Spanish history of America does Otero mention the U.S.-dominated period of New Mexico's history, and he deemphasizes the United States' role as conqueror by presenting New Mexico as social and civilized when U.S. troops arrived during Gen. Stephan Watts Kearney's 1846 invasion of the territory.

While other Nuevomexicano accounts of U.S. military action in New Mexico record the trauma of Kearney's invasion, Otero's Saint Louis World's Fair speech portrays the general's arrival in New Mexico as a social visit rather than an instance of U.S. conquest.[7] Because Kearney was originally from Missouri, Otero tells his audience that the general's arrival created "an additional bond between you and us," and he concludes his account of the U.S. takeover by listing fraternal orders that Missouri officers founded in New Mexico (1904, 2). This presentation of the U.S. conquest contrasts with the Spanish conquest, in which Otero emphasizes the difficulty of establishing "civil and ecclesiastical authority" in a hostile environment (1–2). His history of New Mexico serves to marginalize the United States' role as the bearer of progress and modernity, and his history of Spanish America presents not a romanticized lost Spanish heritage but the foundation for modernity in the region. Spain, and by extension New Mexico, set the infrastructure for contemporary legal practices and urban centers.

In contrast, Otero argues that the United States is guilty of creating a premodern social system in the four remaining territories since the original Louisiana Purchase, calling them "the sole remnants of feudal dependencies, and the ancient un-American theory of the Territories . . . , the unique spectacle of more than one million people, American citizens distributed among four local governing commonwealths, without a voice in national affairs, with no vote in Congress, or an opportunity to ballot for the Chief Magistrate who appoints our Governor and Judges" (1904, 4). Instead of arguing for statehood on the basis that New Mexico has become sufficiently modernized through the expansion of railroads, telephones, or irrigation, Otero claims that the U.S. government has failed to recognize New Mexico's primacy and centrality as a modernizer of North America. In doing so the nation itself has come to embody premodern feudalism.

Otero's assertion that Nuevomexicanos are superior colonizers and his claim that the United States is making them a "unique spectacle" through political disenfranchisement is particularly striking when set within the context of the Louisiana Purchase Exposition. The fair boasted the "most extensive Anthropology Department of any world's fair," headed by William John McGee, a prominent U.S. anthropologist whose biologically based theory of racial hierarchy classified the world's population into "four cultural grades of savagery, barbarism, civilization, and enlightenment" (Rydell 1984, 160–61). His section of the fair featured "living ethnological exhibits" that housed Native Americans, "pygmies from Africa, 'Patagonian giants' from Argentina, [and] Ainu aborigines from Japan." In addition, the U.S. government sponsored an exhibit of more than a thousand Filipino people, highlighting the nation's most recent territorial acquisition from the Spanish-American War (163). Otero wanted to contrast the territorial status of places like the Philippines with that of New Mexico. In fact, he touted New Mexico's contribution to Roosevelt's Rough Riders during the Spanish-American War in numerous political speeches, including his Saint Louis World's Fair speech. The "spectacle" that territorialism makes of New Mexicans is presented in opposition to the spectacle of racial hierarchy so visible in the anthropology exhibits that were held in proximity to the New Mexico Day celebration. Otero's descriptions of New Mexico's participation in the Spanish-American War demonstrate that he is not anti-imperial. Instead, his distinction between modern U.S. empire building in the Pacific and premodern vassalage in the Southwest reveals the underpinnings of race within U.S. concepts of time, progress, and democratic participation. Otero did not want to overturn or even disrupt U.S. modernity; he wanted Nuevomexicanos to be included in it.

The Political Manipulation of New Mexico's Temporality

Otero's attempt to prove that New Mexico was worthy of participatory, democratic self-rule by bringing industrial progress and efficient government to the territory failed to recognize that, for U.S. modernity, modernization *depends* on racialized scales of development. In the late nineteenth century, modernization involved not only increased industrialization and the consolidation of executive political power; it also systemized racism through political actions such as the Supreme Court's endorsement of segregation, the founding of the Immigration Restriction League, and the repeated denial of New Mexican statehood. The second greatest antagonist of Otero's biography, after Thomas Catron, is Senator Albert Beveridge. As chair of the Senate Committee on Territories, Beveridge translated sociological hierarchies of development into political (in)action. Beveridge's rhetoric of racial hierarchies, much like the ethnological exhibits at the world's fair, posited the biological superiority of Anglo-Saxon blood. In addition to chairing the Senate Committee on Territories, Beveridge was a member of the Committee on the Philippines and a key figure in United States' treatment of its territorial holdings. As the man who had described New Mexicans living in mud huts to the Senate in 1902, Albert Beveridge *did* align New Mexico and the Philippines, believing that "both were backward places, burdened by the legacy of Spain's deficiencies, and much effort would be needed 'to save that soil for liberty and civilization'" (qtd. in Holtby 2012, 45). In 1902 he actively fought against New Mexico statehood, and his main weapon was time.

Beveridge's 1898 campaign speech, "March of the Flag," famously championed U.S. imperialism. In it he proclaimed, "The opposition tells us that we ought not to govern a people without their consent. I answer, the rule of liberty that all just government derives its authority from the consent of the governed, applies only to those who are capable of self-government. We govern the Indians without their consent; we govern our territories without their consent; we govern our children without their consent." Here Beveridge's triple parallel between the biological development of a child, the sociological development of a race, and the political development of a region works through linear narratives of progress to infantilize colonized ethnic subjects. Beveridge worked repeatedly against statehood for New Mexico during the twelve years he sat in Congress and especially during his four years as chair of the Senate Committee on Territories.[8] He fought to continue ruling New Mexico without the territory's consent even when a majority of the House and Senate were in favor of granting statehood. The most devastating experience in Otero's fight for statehood occurred during the congressional sessions held in 1902. On May 9 an omnibus bill called the Knox Bill passed the House after only two hours of deliberation. This bill would have admitted Arizona,

Oklahoma, and New Mexico all at once. Residents of all three territories were excited when the bill passed the House so quickly. Once the Knox Bill reached the Senate, however, Beveridge and his committee postponed reviewing it for more than five weeks, explicitly devaluing New Mexicans' time as they awaited the assessment. The Senate session was nearing its conclusion by the time Beveridge seriously examined the bill, and he recommended waiting until the next senate session to vote on it, using delay to wield his power in an act of temporal colonization.

Between sessions Beveridge devised a plan that would prove New Mexico was unfit for admission into the Union. He arranged for a tour of the three territories included in the omnibus bill, focusing mainly on Arizona and New Mexico. Robert Larson convincingly argues that Beveridge orchestrated this inquiry into New Mexico's fitness for statehood, explaining that Beveridge prepared for additional testimony upon his return from the territories but "hesitated" to call on anyone, "unless he knew to what they would testify" (1968, 210). In his autobiography Otero wrote, "I was disgusted with Senator Beveridge as he seemed to be the whole thing [*sic*] and managed the plans . . . to perfection" (1940, 212–13). Beveridge specifically sought the least educated officials for questioning during the inquiry, and according to Otero, Beveridge's assistant, L. G. Rothschild, was directed to photograph drunks and prostitutes to show the "general condition" of New Mexico (218). Beveridge's investigation was clearly contrived. He constructed an image of social and economic underdevelopment to impede the territory's actual development. In a letter to Senator Nelson Aldrich, Beveridge promised to "make an unfavorable impression on the people and investors, which will set the territories back for many years" (qtd. in Holtby 2012, 55). Like corrupt politicians within the territory, Beveridge worked to create the underdevelopment that he would purport was inherent in the region.

The immediate consequence of Beveridge's inquiry was a scathing report on New Mexico and Arizona given to the Senate at the beginning of the second session of the Fifty-Seventh U.S. Congress. Unable to speak in Congress, Otero could do nothing but listen to the report that stated New Mexico and Arizona were not ready for statehood, that the people of New Mexico were uneducated, and that the available irrigation would take at least a generation of research before it could support agriculture.[9] Otero returned to New Mexico while, in the mean time, Beveridge sustained a three-month filibuster of the Knox Bill. Throughout the process Beveridge's key weapon was time. He depicted the territory as premodern and slow to develop in his reports, and he delayed political progress for the territory by repeatedly stalling a vote on the bill. Beveridge's ability to sustain a three-month filibuster against New Mexico statehood exposes the colonial power of the extended mean time during which Nuevomexicanos were denied participation in U.S. modernity.

President Roosevelt also became allied in the suppression of New Mexico statehood and the temporal manipulation it entailed. Roosevelt supported statehood in his initial campaign platform but then reversed his stance while president. In 1906 both Roosevelt and Beveridge came out in support of a bill that would have combined New Mexico and Arizona into one state. The idea of joint statehood had been unpopular in both territories for years. Roosevelt wrote an open letter to Arizona residents encouraging jointure, and it was widely circulated in New Mexico in both Spanish and English: "It is my belief that if the people of Arizona let this chance go by they will have to wait very many years before the chance again offers itself, and even then it will very probably be only upon the present terms—that is, upon the condition of being joined with New Mexico. . . . If they [the people of Arizona] refuse what is profited them . . . they condemn themselves to an indefinite condition of tutelage" (1906, 2). Roosevelt's threat of indefinite territorial dependence was actually a complete fabrication. Only months earlier Roosevelt had written a private letter to B. I. Wheeler, stating, "The only reason I want them [Arizona and New Mexico] in as one state now is that I fear the alternative is having them as two states three or four years hence" (qtd. in Larson 1968, 235).

Otero suspected that New Mexico statehood was eminent, and he fought against joint statehood. But Roosevelt's temporal manipulation was successful in swaying a majority of New Mexicans to vote in favor of jointure (Arizona's vote against joint statehood is what prevented the bill from passing). Roosevelt's maneuver was a culmination of U.S. temporal colonization in New Mexico. The letter threatened to place Arizona and New Mexico eternally outside of U.S. modernity and outside of the political and economic enfranchisement that modern subjectivity promised while placing the onus of this exclusion on New Mexico and Arizona residents themselves. Otero wrote decades later in his autobiography about watching fellow politicians desert the cause of single statehood at this period. Reflecting back on the battle for statehood, he wrote "time was to show that we were right" (1940, 219).

In spite of multiple defeats, Otero maintained faith in time, specifically in the form of time called progress, the idea that linear time moves forward (even if very slowly) into a better future. Despite Otero's faith in progress and modernity, New Mexico continues to exist in a unique temporal junction even in the twenty-first century, aligned with the past and the future, but often struggling for enfranchisement in the present. The process of modernization has blossomed into a substantial science and technology industry that continues to place the state in a federally dependent position with many of the populations' higher-paying jobs housed in two national laboratories, Sandia and Los Alamos, both embroiled in military-weapons design. Los Alamos, New Mexico, is where the atomic bomb was designed and Alamogordo, New Mexico, was the first atomic test site. Thus, New Mexico played a major role in ushering in the atomic age. Perhaps for this reason speculative futures abound in the state as well. New Mexico began building a spaceport in 2012 to launch commercial spacecraft from the site, but six years into the construction it stalled out. The *Atlantic* said of the project, "Spaceport America lies about 20 miles southeast of Truth or Consequences, roughly 50 miles north of Las Cruces, and at a perpetually indeterminate moment in the near future" (Burrington 2018). At the same time the state's tourist industry thrives on marketing New Mexico's cultural history through Indian markets, Spanish plazas, and adobe-style buildings, which, for example, are mandated by Santa Fe's strict architectural codes. New Mexico's uneven relationship with modernity is in small part an inheritance from Miguel Otero, who never quite succeeded at linking the territory to the present of U.S. modernity.

CHAPTER 3

Specters of Recovery

Temporal Economies of Debt and Inheritance in Adina De Zavala's *History and Legends of the Alamo*

Beginning in 1993 a four-year battle was waged over the Alamo Plaza. It was no kitsch reenactment of Davy Crockett and William B. Travis's encounter with General Santa Anna—after all, that battle lasted only thirteen days. No, this battle was waged over the installation of a memorial plaque to honor Adina De Zavala, dubbed the "Angel of the Alamo," when she saved part of the building from demolition in the early twentieth century.[1] De Zavala was also one of the harshest critics of the Daughters of the Republic of Texas (DRT), who became the Alamo's official steward for more than a century. In 1955, shortly after De Zavala's death, the Texas House and Senate passed a resolution ordering that "in her name an appropriate plaque be placed in the Alamo . . . in grateful recognition of her services to the history of Texas," but nothing was done for almost forty years and no plaque bearing Adina De Zavala's name has ever been placed inside the Alamo (Texas Senate 1955, 51). The main debate about whether to create a marker for De Zavala and where to place it was waged between the chair of the Bexar County Historical Commission, Richard Santos, and key members of the DRT. Even after the marker was approved and cast, it sat in the basement of the county courthouse for years and was ultimately placed at a significant distance from the Alamo building.

The *San Antonio Express-News* covered the battle in the midnineties, stating, "The effort to give De Zavala credit for her contributions to Texas has stalled out" (C. Anderson n.d.). Reporting on a celebration of De Zavala's 145th birthday at the Spanish Governor's Palace, which she also helped preserve, the *Express-News* titled an article "Preservationist Adina De Zavala Getting Her Due as Historical Figure" (Ayala 2006). Covering her reemergence as a public figure, the *Express-News*'s terminology reflects the temporal economy of historical recovery. Their language of credit and dues imagines people's relationship to the past as one of debtors to their creditor. But what credit is due to figures from the past? How do you repay a ghost? Adina De Zavala's own historical preservation responds to this question by rejecting the temporal economy of debt—what we owe the past—and replacing it with the logic of inheritance: what the past is giving us and what we must give to the future. She does so by incorporating voices of the dead through an intertextual dialogue of folktales, reports, poems, letters, maps, diaries, and other documents, making the past an open field of engagement rather than a finite object of analysis.

De Zavala's writing self-consciously reflects on the process of preservation and historical recovery. Her account of the Alamo building intervenes in an economy of time that reifies the past through the commodification of historical symbols. De Zavala recounts her struggle for the Alamo building in her 1917 book, *History and Legends of the Alamo and Other Missions in and around San Antonio*. The book is a multigeneric text that brings together historical, literary, and folk accounts of San Antonio's missions and sets them in dialogic relation to one another and to De Zavala's own narratives through thoughtful arrangement. De Zavala's dialogism is very different from María Amparo Ruiz de Burton's novelistic dialogue. Whereas *The Squatter and the Don* excavates the incongruences of U.S. colonization by juxtaposing conflicting forms of U.S. colonial time, De Zavala's dialogism sets up an open-ended interrelation of places, people, and events. Yet both women disrupt smooth, linear narratives of U.S. national development. *History and Legends* confronts U.S. modernity's manipulation of the past by focusing on the complexity and the specificity of people, places, and events above and against their abstract symbolic meaning in popular discourses of Anglo Texan superiority.

De Zavala significantly altered the landscape of San Antonio by spearheading the preservation of numerous Spanish buildings in and around the city, pushing for the retention of Spanish street names, and campaigning for public schools to be named after Texas's historical figures. Her work also refigured the city's timescape by opening San Antonio's historical narrative to neglected voices of the past and future. Her historical writing does not trace a debt to the past or an investment in cultural capital. Instead, it proposes relationships among historical material and spectral voices that disrupt presentist designs on the Alamo and other historical sites in the San Antonio area. Philosopher Jacques Derrida reflects on the temporality of specters in *Archive Fever* (1996) and *Specters of Marx* (1994), his own engagement with the ghosts of Sigmund Freud and Karl Marx, respectively. Neither past nor present, specters signify absence but are not fully absent, and according to Derrida, they disjoin time. Though not a philosopher, and predating Derrida by half a century, De Zavala, through her writing and archival collections, models the work of learning to live with ghosts that Derrida presents as an ethics of deconstruction. He writes, "The time of the 'learning to live,' a time without tutelary presence, would amount to this . . . : to learn to live with ghosts, in the upkeep, the conversation, the company, or the companionship, in *the commerce without commerce of ghosts*. . . . And this being-with specters would also be, not only but also, a politics of memory, of inheritance, and of generations" (1994, xvii–xviii; italics added).

The politics of memory, inheritance, and generations is also a politics of time. De Zavala's text performs a being-with-ghosts that disrupts modernity's linear history and participates in a relationship of inheritance and responsibility to those not present and those denied presence by U.S. modernity. Adina De Zavala worked to share the cultural, political, historical, and architectural inheritance of San Antonio with the community that lived there, contra the politics of debt. Her work critiques U.S. modernity's economically driven historical preservation that views conservation as an investment with an expected return. Her writing and preservation resist capitalism's abstraction of time by emphasizing the material and historical specificity of people, places, and documents over and against attempts to commodify them. In doing so she disrupts the homogeneity of time on which capitalist value depends and creates a dialogic relation to the past that undermines modernity's linear temporality. The fact that De Zavala's narrative form resists capitalist abstraction does not mean she was anticapitalist in her personal financial transactions. Like Ruiz de Burton and Miguel Antonio Otero, De Zavala was a descendent of the elite landed gentry of Mexico and New Spain. She and her siblings profited from the rent and sale of land they had jointly inherited. Yet De Zavala's anticapitalist historiography of communal inheritance is actually visible across a number of early elite Mexican American authors. For example, Marissa López's account of Mariano Vallejo describes his historical writing in contrast to Herbert H. Bancroft, who produced California history in the nineteenth century through an unnamed industrialized workforce of writers and catalogers, advertising his history as the "wealth of nations." Californio patriarch Don Mariano Vallejo, in contrast, describes history as "*el testigo de los tiempos*" and "*el mensajero de la antigüedad*" in his personal narrative (qtd. in López 2007, 878). López argues, "The distinction between Bancroft's and Vallejo's philosophies of history [is]: history as a function of the economic consolidation of national identity, and as a rhetorical link to the past. In the former position, Anglo-American nationalism is tied to the efficiency of capitalist modes of production and the integration of the national economy in post–Civil War America" (879). Vallejo's personification of history as *el testigo* (a witness) and *el mensajero* (a messenger) also invokes a spectral relationship to the past. Thus, De Zavala's work is part of a broader historical imaginary among Mexican American authors that resists reification and temporal homogeneity. Unlike Vallejo's anthropomorphized history, though, De Zavala's specters are the individual ghostly figures attached to specific material places and documents.

De Zavala's folktale, "The Padre's Gift," sheds light on the structure of *History and Legends* and on her broader world of preservation and collection. One way De Zavala traces routes of inheritance is by describing the transfer of historical records and examining the way that old archives become incorporated into new ones. "The Padre's Gift" allegorizes the movement of archives. The first-person narrator of the tale describes her encounter with "the padre," a folk figure who appears in the community across generations to offer gifts, like a bag of Spanish doubloons or "the deed to land [that a] family had long lost" (1996, 54). When she encounters the padre at a well, he gives her an ancient book made of parchment. She asks if she may have it translated from its original Spanish, but he replies, "No, use what you can and pass it on. Promise that no hand but yours shall touch this gift until it is bequeathed by you as I now bequeath it to you." Though the padre enjoins the speaker "that no hand [but hers] shall touch" the book while she lives, the woman is, herself, a communal figure; "we all know you," the padre says when he greets her (56). Thus, her job is not to hoard the book as an object of private property but to safeguard it for future inheritors. The padre provides no instructions about how to use or interpret his gift, leaving it to an open-ended indeterminate future. The content of the padre's book is never described (much like Edgar Allan Poe's infamous "Purloined Letter"). In fact, the narrator's ability to read the book is not important to the padre; what matters is her ability to preserve it and pass it on to another, unknown, future recipient. "The Padre's Gift" is about the circulation and preservation of archives rather than their fixed meaning.

Yet the material specificity of the padre's book is important, as he commands the narrator to leave it untranslated. Writing about Latina/o archive formation, Rodrigo Lazo explains that translation can "integrate marginalized and forgotten people even as it threatens to alter the content of the migrant archive and erase, however gently, language difference," but he also argues that there is something of the original language that exists as a trace even in the translation (2010, 201). De Zavala's insistence on the untranslatable material specificity of the archive in "The Padre's Gift" at the expense of integration and even intelligibility is paradoxically what makes her archive spectral. Fredric Jameson asserts that spectrality "is designed to undermine the very ideology of spirit itself. Ghosts are thus in that sense material; ghosts very precisely resist the strategies of sublimation let alone those of idealization" (1999, 52). De Zavala's specters emerge from the material specificity of her archives to resist the abstraction of capitalist exchange, placing them outside the temporal economy of debt. De Zavala has no interest in the spirit of the Alamo or any other mission; she is interested in its messy, unsightly, precise past.

Her interest in the spectral circulation of archival material is not confined to the legends portion of her book. In *History and Legends*' historical section about the Alamo, De Zavala juxtaposes the progress of land tenure with the transference of archival documents. Describing church records from Mission San Antonio de Valero (which would later be called the Alamo), De Zavala quotes a record of the eighteenth-century resettlement of Adaeseños from current day Louisiana to the Texas mission: "In fact of having found themselves royally in possession, etc., and by the same [the land] is given to them that they may take it and profit thereby, they, their heirs and successors . . ." (1996, 8). Immediately after the ellipsis De Zavala moves to a discussion of the transfer of church records during secularization, quoting at length the affidavits of transfer between various clergy in 1793, 1794, and 1804. The ellipsis signals an aporia of U.S. colonial (un)settlement—when Spanish colonists are resettled from Los Adaes to San Antonio, where their "heirs and successors" would later be dispossessed by Anglo-Americans—but the ellipsis also leads to a new link across time through archival transmission. By including the Alamo mission's record of archival transfer, De Zavala also symbolically includes *History and Legends* in that network of transmission. Like "The Padre's Gift," this textual organization involves her in a dialogic relationship with specters. Her preservation establishes a communal link to the past at a moment when Tejano connection through space has been uprooted by U.S. colonization. She builds an archival record across time to supplement the aporia of land loss and spatial displacement.

These sections of *History and Legends* implicate De Zavala as a specter of the archive in her own right by linking her to the ghostly record keepers she depicts in folklore and history. Her unacknowledged impact on the landscape of San Antonio establishes her as an absent presence within the city. At the same time her work invisibly shaped the written history of Texas. Robert Ables's 1955 MA thesis on De Zavala remains the only book-length account of her life. In it Ables includes an interview with De Zavala's friend Mrs. W. J. Simmons, who explained, "She was the source of information of many articles contributed to Texas history, for which she received no *credit*. This I know very well, being a visitor in her home when students and historians of note would be there seeking information. And always in her amiable, unselfish manner she would respond to their call. She was never too busy, or otherwise engaged, to give information of historic *value*" (112; italics added). Like the *San Antonio Express-News*, Simmons frames De Zavala's intellectual contributions through the logic of debt. Yet, as specter, De Zavala disrupts the linear time of credit and debt. This chapter seeks not to pay De Zavala her due as an important historical influence in Texas but to engage with her as an interlocutor who contributes to a theory of the archive. Her work lays a path out of the temporal economy of debt and toward an open-ended dialogic engagement with past and future voices.

The Logic of Debt and the Temporal Economy of Literary Recovery

The colonial threat of historical erasure functions through financial and psychosocial economies of time. The financial economy of history involves the price of purchasing, organizing, and housing archival material, as well as the cost of constructing and distributing knowledge about the past. The financial economy that produces history is deeply intertwined with a psychosocial economy that assigns differing value to events, people, material, and locations across time. Psychosocial economies traffic in cultural capital—knowledge, aesthetics, and performative acts that translate into race, class, and gender identity and power. This connection makes archives and archivization a key technology of U.S. modernity's racialized forms of time. De Zavala's preservation work in San Antonio and the work done to recover her life and writing expose the inner workings of U.S. modernity's temporal economy in relation to both financial and cultural commodification.

De Zavala's work was recovered by Richard Flores, who edited and introduced *History and Legends*, which was republished by Arte Público's Recovering the U.S. Hispanic Literary Heritage project in 1996. Nicolás Kanellos, director and founder of Arte Público, provides an account of the financial economy that threatens literary recovery: "Recovering the U.S. Hispanic Literary Heritage was turned down repeatedly for funding for many years by the NHPRC [National Historic Publications and Records Commission] and the NEH [National Endowment for the Humanities] while these agencies poured millions of dollars into projects to footnote the papers of the 'founding fathers'" (2012, 373). Here a reifying process of commodification assigns the same degraded economic value to Latina/o culture and history as it does to Latina/o bodies. The U.S. economy devalues multiple iterations of Latina/o time, from physical labor to creative production and philosophical engagement. Kanellos also describes the way that the recovery project has entered into economic relationships with private companies such as Newsbank and EBSCO that charge subscription fees for their databases, placing a monetary value on recovered material and leaving individual universities to decide whether or not they should pay large fees for "minority" texts (374).

The temporal economy of recovery also works through the logic of debt on a symbolic level. The Recovering the U.S. Hispanic Literary Heritage project is funded by a number of philanthropic organizations, including the Rockefeller Foundation, the National Endowment for the Arts, and the Andrew W. Mellon Foundation, among others. Private and government institutions like these are invested in maintaining the neoliberal status quo that keeps them operating. They often employ the rhetoric of multiculturalism—a superficial homage to diversity that deflects effective criticism of the neoliberal state's structural dependence on racism, classism, and sexism.[2] Kirsten Silva Gruesz describes the relation between multiculturalism and literary recovery, writing: "Revision of the U.S. literary canon, as practiced by the multiculturalism of the late 1980s, aims to accommodate Latino cultural memory through an additive process, by juxtaposing (for instance) Mariano Vallejo with Melville to acknowledge that they jointly inhabited a continent and, eventually, a country" (2002, 210). In this light historical recovery places disparate individuals in the "meanwhile" of a Benedict Anderson–style imagined national community (25), fitting Latinas/os into a U.S. national paradigm without altering the underlying structure of racialized time. Similarly, while philanthropy does not entail a financial debt, it is often given with the expectation that recipients will not participate in radical political engagement. For example, in 2004 the American Civil Liberties Union decided to turn down a $1.5 million grant from the Rockefeller Foundation because it contained vague language that required recipients to "not promote or engage in violence, terrorism, bigotry or the destruction of any state" at a time when restrictive immigration laws and the restriction of civil liberties were being coded as "anti-terrorist" in the United States (Strom 2004). Thus, while founders of Recovering the

U.S. Hispanic Literary Heritage may have envisioned a radical revision of literary history and all its social implications, the project's benefactors were not invested in radicalism or revolutionary thought.

In its attempt to give long overdue credit to Latina/o authors of the past who bestowed an artistic and intellectual inheritance on peoples of the United States, the recovery project becomes figuratively indebted to philanthropic organizations—a debt paid not in money but though the psychosocial economy of acknowledgment and gratitude. The copyright page of each volume of the project's book series, Recovering the U.S. Hispanic Literary Heritage, and most of their (re)published historical texts proclaims, "This volume is made possible through grants from . . . the Rockefeller Foundation."[3] The U.S. temporal economy that credits the Rockefeller Foundation for recovering Latina/o texts, yet failed for decades to credit De Zavala for her contributions to Texas history, is inherently uneven in its recognition of debts to the past.

U.S. modernity's capitalist economy functions through empty, homogenous time and transforms people, places, and events into abstract, interchangeable exchange values. Similarly, U.S. modernity's temporal economy structures scholarly and institutional questions such as "How much should we pay for a text to be preserved and republished?" or "How much time should we spend studying a particular text?" and ultimately pits the "value" of Anglo-American forefathers against Latina/o authors. (This economy is quite familiar to scholars who must argue for the value of their intellectual work in various grant applications.) Kanellos writes in the inaugural volume of the Recovering the U.S. Hispanic Literary Heritage series that the Rockefeller funding was "a natural result of the work that the scholars represented in this volume have been developing over a twenty-year period" (1993, 13). Yet the Rockefeller Foundation's choice to fund the project was also likely a calculated investment in a timely cultural and intellectual commodity that would add to the foundation's own political clout in light of the United States' growing Latina/o population.

De Zavala's preservation work almost a century earlier also left her embroiled in the financial economy of historical recovery. Her battle over the Alamo buildings reveals the way that capital investment can colonize the past. De Zavala spearheaded the move to preserve the Alamo buildings in 1902, when she was president of San Antonio's first DRT chapter, the De Zavala Daughters (named after Adina's grandfather, Lorenzo de Zavala). She explains in *History and Legends* that in 1900 "the people of San Antonio had looked upon the old Alamo building as public property for years" (1996, 41). In the late 1800s the Catholic Church sold the Alamo church building to the state of Texas, and the rest of the Alamo property, including the *convento*, or "long barracks," where much of the historic Alamo battle occurred, went to a man named Honoré Grenet. Grenet restored and reconstructed the *convento* with wooden porticos and supposedly planned to donate the building to the public, but he died before his plans were executed. His part of the Alamo property was sold to Hugo and Schmeltzer Firm in 1892, and De Zavala approached the company's owner, Gustav Schmeltzer, immediately, asking that he give the De Zavala DRT chapter the first option to purchase the building when the company was ready to sell. After several more visits from De Zavala over the next eight years, the Hugo and Schmeltzer Firm agreed to sell the building to the DRT for $75,000.

Though the DRT was promised the first option on the property, De Zavala learned that a company from the East wanted to purchase the building and turn it into a hotel. In an expedited effort to raise funds, De Zavala recruited Clara Driscoll, daughter of a wealthy Texas entrepreneur, to join the cause and contribute funds for the building's purchase. Unbeknownst to De Zavala, Driscoll held radically different ideas about the purpose of restoring the Alamo building as a public space. Driscoll wanted to demolish the long barracks, which she thought were unsightly, and replace them with a park that would emphasize the aesthetics of the Alamo church. De Zavala and Driscoll's disagreement led to a feud that split the DRT chapter into two autonomous factions that fought over possession of the building. De Zavala is perhaps best known for barricading herself in the Alamo long barracks for three days in 1908 to prevent their destruction.[4] She ultimately left the DRT and founded the Texas Historical Landmarks Association in 1912, which focused on marking and preserving historic sites throughout San Antonio and the surrounding area. The DRT's construction of the Alamo as a modern monument and De Zavala's competing vision for the building reveal the way that capitalist forms of time dominate projects of historical recovery.

De Zavala's preservation plans focused on historical specificity above and against abstract meaning, whereas Driscoll's vision for the site focused on adding economic value to the city through aesthetic beauty and the cultural commodity of Anglo Texan heroism.

The DRT ultimately produced the Alamo as an abstract, aesthetic space that contributed to both the ideology of Anglo Texan supremacy and the commercial value of San Antonio. The destruction of the long barracks was part of a modernist aesthetic project to transform the Alamo through a modernity that "produc[es] the old as remorselessly as it produces the new, and in equal measure" (Osborne 1996, xii). The DRT's Alamo created a sacred space of communal memory at the service of commercialism. The Alamo became an idealized symbol of history that could be copied and reproduced like, for example, Alamo-shaped paperweights sold in the monument's gift shop. Driscoll (n.d.) specifically sought donations from Texas hotel managers "to improve the surroundings [of the Alamo church], so that they may be in keeping with the dignity and glory of the old ruin." Her project of "improvement" was a planned demolition of the long barracks that would produce the Alamo as a discrete space surrounded by a park within the newly developed commercial center of San Antonio. The donations from local hotel managers were actually a kind of investment made with the expectation that the DRT's improvements would beautify the city and increase tourist and business traffic.

Hotel managers' donations were also an investment in the construction of Anglo Texan superiority, which went hand in hand with Anglo economic domination in the city and the state. Flores (2002) details this process in *Remembering the Alamo*. The ideological development of the Alamo building as a site of Anglo-American patriotism worked toward a seamless narrative of Anglo-American superiority that, Flores explains, reified Anglo and Mexican identity by depicting the two races in binary opposition as heroes and villains of the Alamo battle, respectively. Driscoll wanted to create a "worthy and artistic monument" to the hero-martyrs of the Alamo battle, as she wrote in her letter to Texas hotel managers. But Driscoll's own published literary account of the battle made "no attempt to present the complexities of the past in relation to Texan and Mexican social history and assumes, quite incorrectly, that the defenders of the Alamo were all U.S. citizens or 'Texans'" (Flores 2002,

72). Driscoll showed no interest in remembering the actual men who fought in the Alamo but instead wanted to graft the Alamo battle onto a narrative of Anglo-American triumph as part of the fulfillment of Manifest Destiny. Driscoll's wealthy father was part of the Anglo-American class that reshaped San Antonio by shifting the commercial center away from the Mexican-dominated Main and Military Plazas and toward the area surrounding the Alamo building.[5] Like the Texas hotel managers, Clara Driscoll's interest in preserving the Alamo was an investment in her own class and race status.

In contrast, De Zavala's vision for the Alamo was based on material specificity that resisted the kind of historical commodity fetishism and ethnic reification evident in Driscoll's plan. Classically defined, *commodity fetishism* transforms the social characteristics of labor into a relationship between things (commodities), but I want to propose the concept of *historical commodity fetishism*, which transforms the materially specific characteristics of an event in time and space into a relationship between abstract symbols of sociocultural value. De Zavala fought against the historical commodity fetishism that would come to alienate the Alamo from its community in San Antonio. In her own letter to the people of Texas, De Zavala uses a competing patriotic rhetoric to rail against "the Hotel Syndicate and many property owners adjacent to the old Alamo" who would benefit from the destruction of the long barracks (De Zavala n.d.a), and her animated account of the dispute in *History and Legends* proclaims, "Long the battle waged—it was De Zavala Daughters versus Commercialism! New combinations and new syndicates were formed from time to time as new interests entered the contests to destroy the Alamo proper. . . . The methods used by the interests are almost unbelievable!" (1996, 46). De Zavala's attempt to purchase the Alamo long barracks ironically rested on a desire to remove the building from the realm of capitalist exchange. Her interest in the Alamo differed from syndicate interests that expected a financial return on their investment in Texas history. Her plan for the long barracks reflected a belief that history is a communal inheritance and focused on the material specificity of that inheritance.

While Driscoll (n.d.) wanted to transform the Alamo into a "worthy monument," De Zavala planned to restore the long barracks and use them as a "Hall of Fame and a Museum of History, Relics, Art and Literature" (1996, 45).

The plan for a monument versus that of a museum reflect the two women's different uses of time. The temporality of a monument is flat. It stages the simplistic immediacy of a connection between past and present, much like Paul Earlie's Derridian description of debt, which "intellectual, financial or otherwise, always involves a certain repression of the movement of spacing" and "implies the identical repetition of a trace," the past instantiated in the present (2015, 314). A museum, in contrast, is what Michel Foucault refers to as a "heterochrony" (the temporal version of a heterotopia) that brings together multiple forms of time (1986, 6–7). Museums assemble materially specific artifacts and place them in conversation with one another, visually, if not textually. While Driscoll's vision for the Alamo embodied the two-dimensional reification of Anglo and Mexican identity that Flores (2002) expertly describes in *Remembering the Alamo*, De Zavala actively fought the Alamo's transformation into a symbol of anti-Mexican sentiment. According to her own words, she did not want the building to be a symbol at all. In a 1936 letter to the editor, again defending the importance of the Alamo long barracks, she recounts the Battle of the Alamo: "They tell us that this does not matter; that all we need is a symbol for the people to rave over; that the Alamo church answers that purpose—that we do not have to have even the approximate truth of the facts—or the real thing!" While De Zavala's plans for the Alamo were never realized, she built into her textual rendering of the site what she was unable to construct materially.

Her account of the building in *History and Legends* is not a direct, linear narrative. She presents a compilation of texts and images from a wide range of historical documents, including Spanish colonial records about the construction and condition of the building, a letter to Sam Houston from chief engineer Green B. Jameson about the plan of the building, letters from William Barrett Travis about the prospects of the Alamo battle, and the signed testimony of Gustav Schmeltzer about the transfer of the building to the DRT. Not only that, she refers to defenders of the Alamo as Texans, not Americans, and includes a list of men who died in the Alamo with their country or U.S. state of birth listed, when known. De Zavala's close attention to textual detail leads her to recognize the indeterminacy of the past. For example, she explains, "Potter and other historians give fourteen as the number of guns used [in the Alamo battle], Mrs. Dickenson said there were eighteen, and Green B. Jameson and Santa Anna placed the number at twenty-one" (1996, 18). She notably credits the sources of her information, incorporating the divergent accounts of historians, a woman witness, and men from each side of the battle. Her concern for the material specificity of the building and the battle push against Driscoll's capitalist aestheticization and decontextualization of the physical space surrounding the Alamo that capitalized on a constructed Anglo-American communal memory.

De Zavala's depiction of the Alamo is no less patriotic or celebratory than that of her rival DRT chapter, but it is significantly less marketable because the complexity and historical specificity of her account make it difficult to reproduce and circulate. She proclaims, in patriotic and paternalistic fashion, "The greatest heritage of the children of Texas and America is the noble example of its great men heroes. Let us not forget their deathless deeds," but her emphasis on remembering the specific details of not only the battle but the entire history of the Alamo resists the abstract valorization of Anglo Texas and incorporates a variety of transnational, Tejano, and women's voices (1996, 36). She presents the people involved in the building's transformation across time not as symbols but as individuals, accessible through the words they wrote and spoke. Her description of events defines Texas and Texans as separate from the United States, which they were at the time of the Alamo battle. In this way her patriotic rhetoric either celebrates Texas nationalism contra to U.S. nationalism or demands that U.S. nationalism recognize its own transnational origins. In *History and Legends*' folklore section, De Zavala presents Alamo defenders not like the hero-martyrs of Driscoll's account but as ghosts with flaming swords who stake their claim on the building and guard against its destruction even in the present.

De Zavala's communal imagining of the building works to remove it from the realm of market exchange and the colonial temporality of debt. In her open letter about the Alamo, De Zavala (n.d.a) discusses the New York–based hotel syndicate attempting to buy the long barracks, asking, "Shall alien gold dictate to Texans how they shall care for their Alamo?" Capitalist exchange, if not always alien, is at least alienating, as it transforms social relationships into financial transactions. Debt is the gap in value that supports colonial power structures by appearing to create equivalencies while actually perpetuating inequity. In theory debtors can cancel their debt merely by repaying it, but in practice systems of debt are neither transparent nor equitable. Global capitalism works by installing systems of unequal exchange and siphoning off the surplus value of colonized labor. The previous chapters have presented case studies in the production of underdevelopment on which capitalist development depends. Colonial (and neocolonial) capitalism produces a system of perpetual debt and dependence to enforce colonial difference through racial inequity. For example, the transfer of northern Mexico to the United States through the Treaty of Guadalupe Hidalgo was compensated by a payment of $15 million to Mexico and the cancellation of Mexican debt to the United States, but the United States continues to hold Mexican debt, due in part to the legacy of lost territorial assets and political instability perpetuated by the U.S.-Mexico War. Mexican Americans' land dispossession occurred after the U.S.-Mexico War, when U.S. citizens of Mexican descent were forced to pay legal fees and other debts with their land, thus extending the supposedly paid "Mexican debt" indefinitely into a future of economic disparity.

The unequal exchange and devaluation of colonized subjects in the U.S. Southwest is both material and ideological. Racialized temporal economies perform financial, political, and moralizing functions. In the context of colonization, debt is a structural position, not just a temporary situation. Indeed, De Zavala's own class privilege stemmed from Spanish colonial systems of debt peonage, perhaps the most literal example of structural debt. As with Otero and Ruiz de Burton, De Zavala's writing signals a preoccupation with Mexican Americans' altered colonial status rather than the underlying global system of coloniality. Once lost, Tejano inheritance is transformed into an unpayable debt. The alien(ating) gold of East Coast investors would not have placed a fixed value on the Alamo building that could be easily transferred back to Texas. Instead, it threatened to remove the Alamo from local, communal control and create an alienating space out of Texas's historical site.

After Driscoll gained control of both the Alamo long barracks and the San Antonio DRT, De Zavala disbanded the De Zavala chapter of the DRT and formed the Texas Historical Landmarks Association. She spearheaded the preservation of the Spanish Governor's Palace, having learned from her experience with the Alamo building. The association outlined exactly what credit would be given to donors of $1,000 or more—their name would be included on a bronze plaque—and stipulated that the association trustees would maintain control of the building (De Zavala n.d.b). This contract-like solicitation for donations guarded against wealthy donors who might seek control of the Spanish Governor's Palace the way that Driscoll gained control of the Alamo.

Despite the association's clearly demarcated authority outlined in De Zavala's solicitation for donations, her description of how the Spanish Governor's Palace would be used was open-ended and in dialogue with the community. She explains, "It is intended that this building when saved shall be devoted to the needs of the people; to care for their history, past, present and future; to preserve relics—yes—but also to serve the city, county, state, and Nation as best may be in time of stress, is the aim of its promoters. The plans are not limited, but unlimited service" (De Zavala n.d.b). The "time of stress" that De Zavala mentions may have been a reference to World War I, which the United States had not yet entered when she began her campaign to save the Spanish Governor's Palace in 1915. But World War I would certainly not have been the first "time of stress" for South Texas. A palimpsest of Spanish, Mexican, French, and U.S. colonial systems created a space where different forms of time comingled and collided within Texas. De Zavala's conceptualization of history as "past, present and future" (rather than just past) pushes against modernity's abstract historical commodity fetishism by including multiple forms of time, especially those yet to be defined: a future history. Texas's complex, discontinuous iterations of time provide the ground for the "unlimited service" of De Zavala's preserved Spanish Governor's Palace by setting the past, present, and future in an ongoing dialogic relationship. The mobilized, heterogeneous history De Zavala imagines is grounded in material specificity. Just as her criticism of the DRT resisted their production of an abstract reified aesthetic for the Alamo building, her plans for the Spanish Governor's Palace remained responsive to the spatially and temporally situated "needs of the people."

Archival Violence and the Complex Inheritance of Latinidad

De Zavala's experiences with the Alamo illustrate the way that sociocultural effects of archive formation are deeply interrelated with economies of capitalist distribution. In *Archive Fever* Derrida proposes that systems of classification deny the fullness and complexity of meaning for archival materials by projecting a false unity: "The gathering into itself of the One is never without violence. . . . At once, at the same time, but in a same time that is out of joint, the One forgets to remember itself to itself, it keeps and erases this injustice that it is" (1996, 78). The process of archival selection and exclusion also does violence to the people, objects, and identities that remain outside the archive, as exemplified in Kanellos's (2012) critique of U.S. archives' exclusion of Hispanic-authored texts. The false unity created by the economy of archival selection and exclusion has important psychosocial ramifications. It produces a self-alienating identity, as the "one forgets to remember itself to itself" (Derrida 1996, 78). What Derrida does not explicitly address is that the material process of archivization often depends on financial transactions and thus archival alienation and capitalist alienation are mutually constitutive.

Lazo (2010) draws on Derrida to describe the archival violence performed in the selection and exclusion of what he calls "migrant archives"—material that has been historically excluded but is now moving into official archival spaces. John-Michael Rivera, who discusses archival encounters, also engages Derridian theory. He recounts his childhood experience discovering a treasure trove of material in the apartment of Mr. Martinez: teacher, volunteer librarian, and unofficial archivist of "Latino culture in the San Fernando Valley, the place where he was born and would die." When neither professional librarians nor his own community invested the time and money to save Martinez's collection, Rivera's "belief in the power of things, in things Latino, began to lose its significance and appeal," and he "began to see [the cultural objects] as junk" (2007, 1–2). The experience of archival exclusion caused him to internalize self-alienating values of market capitalism. Despite the migration of Latina/o cultural material into traditional archives and the development of new archives that value work like Mr. Martinez's, the unity or cohesion that organizes archives in the United States and other Western nations continue to be structured by the model of self-legitimating white, bourgeois citizen subjectivity.

Derrida does not explicitly link *Archive Fever*'s engagement with psychoanalysis and *Specters of Marx*'s economic critique, nor do Rivera or Lazo. But

Derrida's treatises on Freud and Marx both illuminate modernity's relationship to the past by exploring issues of inheritance, spectrality, and disjointed time. Capitalist and psychoanalytic forms of time operate in a temporal economy of debt. Debt is an inscription—a trace—that repeats the past in the present. The temporal logic of debt structures the present through an originary event—be it an act of patriarchal founding, national origin, capitalist financing, or psychological trauma—that must be addressed in the present, often through repetition. The concept of debt contrasts the Derridian idea of inheritance, a future-focused "open incalculability," as Earlie describes it, which engenders transformation rather than repetition (2015, 314). Adina De Zavala's historical preservation focuses on the temporality of inheritance rather than debt, as evident in the unlimited service she articulates for the Spanish Governor's Palace and the unspecified use for "The Padre's Gift." Like her material preservation work, De Zavala's *History and Legends* shifts historiography from debt to inheritance through its dialogic juxtaposition of historical material and, especially, through its inclusion of folkloric specters that disrupt the metaphysics of presence and historical objectivity.

The psychosocial economy of debt that De Zavala moves away from, ironically, resurfaces in the 1996 recovery of her work, which reads De Zavala's writing as an ethnic displacement. Flores argues, "The crux of my thesis on De Zavala is that her deep interest in the material and social restoration of a Spanish and Mexican past, expressed through her work of artifactual preservation and historical legendry, results from the displacement of her 'Mexican' self onto these other levels of practice. . . . Her life is spent in search of the 'lost realms' of Spanish and Mexican Texas precisely because her ethnic sense of self has been displaced by Texas subjectivity" (1996, xlviii). This reading of repression repeats the temporal logic of the DRT's suppression of her historical work. The unity of the subject (be it psychological or ethnic), like the unity of the archive, is a form of violence. Antonio Viego describes the systemic implications of ego-psychology for Latinx studies: "Critical race and ethnicity studies scholars have developed no language to talk about ethnic-racialized subjectivity and experience that is not entirely ego- and social psychological and that does not imagine a strong, whole, complete, and transparent ethnic-racialized subject and ego as the desired therapeutic, philosophical and political outcome in a racist, white supremacist world. In the process, we fail to see how the repeated themes of wholeness, completeness, and transparency with respect to ethnic-racialized subjectivity are what provide racist discourse with precisely the notion of subjectivity that it needs to function most effectively" (2007, 4) The critique that De Zavala ignored contemporary Mexican Americans also belies an assumption that the present should be the privileged temporal sphere, that De Zavala should have been more concerned with the material conditions of Mexican Americans in her present than with the material buildings and documents of the past, and that the parts of history most valued by the present analyst/scholar should be most valued in the past as well.

The political foment in South Texas that was contemporary to, yet outside of, De Zavala's work is the past to which Flores assigns a cultural debt for Chicana/o letters. John-Michael Rivera describes the ethnic debt to and concomitant repression of a proto-Chicana/o revolutionary history that spanned from the 1915 Plan de San Diego to the 1930s work of Communist Party activist Emma Tenayuca. Rivera asserts that "radical emancipation remains a specter in Mexican peoplehood" and that the "Mexican American generation"—parents to the Chicano generation—"emerges ... by repressing its radical past" (2006, 152, 154). Rivera argues that Mexican American identity is constituted by an ambivalence between (1) the collective celebration of its radical past and (2) the collective repression of that radicalism to pursue the illusive promise of U.S. democratic inclusion (147). De Zavala, however, fits neither the paradigm of celebration nor of repression. The Mexican American radical *past* of South Texas occurred during the later years of De Zavala's adult life and is neither the conscious nor the unconscious content of her preservation work. It might help to remember that Adina De Zavala, born in 1861, was actually closer in age to María Amparo Ruiz de Burton than she was to Jovita González or Américo Paredes.[6] If De Zavala's work has a radical past at all, it is the radical past of the Texas Revolution.

Repaying a debt to the Chicana/o specter of radical emancipation by recuperating Adina De Zavala turns out to be impossible. Debt-based recovery paradigms combine normative narratives of ethnoracial development with psychological development. The racial binary of Anglo versus Mexican that dominated historical interpretation (and lived experience) in Texas for more than a century imagines both groups through a fundamentally heteropatriarchal lens of national and ethnic development. Flores describes De Zavala's public persona as "that of a woman of partial Mexican ancestry whose allegiance and politics lie not with her grandfather's 'patria,' but with the emerging Anglo American status quo of the day" (1996, xxix). While Flores reads in De Zavala's text a desire for the restoration of a romantic "Tejas" past, his recovery of her performs its own kind of restoration (2002, 91). By uncovering the Mexican identity that is repressed in her work, Flores symbolically restores that identity (1996, xlvii). Restoration works through the logic of debt by defining an originary loss that can then, supposedly, be equalized. The psychoanalysis of De Zavala is what makes her recoverable as a *mexicana* author (albeit a repressed one), because only by being repressed can De Zavala be restored as a figure of Chicana or *mexicana* cultural production.[7]

The *patria* of her supposed patriarch, grandfather Lorenzo de Zavala, also projects a falsely transparent line of familial and national descent. Both De Zavala's claim to Texas heritage and Flores's recovery of her Mexican identity hinge specifically on her association with Lorenzo de Zavala. She names her DRT chapter after him, and he is the only ancestor whose biography appears in *History and Legends*. But neither Lorenzo de Zavala's national identity nor Adina De Zavala's familial relation to him is linear and transparent. Lorenzo died when Adina's father, Augustine, was only five, after which Augustine was raised by his mother, Emily West de Zavala, and her second husband, a German immigrant named Henry M. Fock. After the death of her third husband, an Anglo Texan, Emily moved to Augustine's home, where she lived during Adina's childhood. Augustine's wife—Adina's mother—was the Irish-born Julia Tyrell. The specificity of Adina De Zavala's familial history troubles the spirit of her Mexican identity much like the specificity of material in *History and Legends* troubles the spirit of the Alamo as an abstract symbol of Anglo Texan superiority.

Lorenzo de Zavala's national identity is no less complex and multifaceted than Adina's connection to him. Flores describes Lorenzo specifically as a "Mexican statesman" (1996, vii), but John-Michael Rivera explains, "In many ways he was never fully a native of any land. . . . Zavala was ironically a man without a people" (2005, xxix). Born a criollo in New Spain, Lorenzo de Zavala was a political representative for Yucatán under both Spanish and Mexican rule. He helped draft the Mexican Constitution of 1824 but was exiled in 1830 for his Federalist politics, and he later helped draft the constitution of the Republic of Texas, serving as that nation's first vice president. These details may appear to be minor, but what is at stake is the very formation of Latinidad. As Lazo explains, "An ethnicity and an ethnic archive validate and sustain each other" (2010, 213). Latinidad is itself complex and multifaceted, spanning an entire hemisphere, rooted in multiple interrelated colonialisms, revolutions, and migrations. Lorenzo de Zavala's national identity, Adina De Zavala's familial heritage, and her historical writing all disrupt notions of cohesive, linear development and abstract, sociocultural value, reflecting a transnational history that is anything but linear. Though Adina De Zavala draws on her biological and national link to the Texas statesman, Lorenzo de Zavala, it is his mobile, discontinuous, multifaceted identity that forms Adina De Zavala's intellectual inheritance.

Learning to Live with Ghosts

De Zavala turns away from linear historical narratives and abstract historical commodity fetishism by creating an intertextual dialogue with the past— indeed, with multiple pasts—and with the future. A large portion of *History and Legends* is composed of other people's writing: church records, poems, letters, lists, photographs, and communally constructed legends. The texts that make up her tome are literally and figuratively full of ghosts. In contrast to ontological literary recovery, which explores a historical figure's identity, De Zavala's work is *hauntological*, a mode of inquiry that Colin Davis describes as the "structural openness or address directed towards the living by the voices of the past or the not yet formulated possibilities of the future." Unlike a gothic or uncanny haunting in which the "ghost's secret" is a "puzzle to be solved" (2005, 378–79), Davis writes, "conversing with specters is not undertaken in the expectation that they will reveal some secret, shameful or otherwise. Rather, it may open us up to the experience of secrecy as such: an essential unknowing which underlies and may undermine what we think we know" (377). De Zavala enacts unknowing through her engagement with the Texas history that has been occluded by hegemonic Anglo-American narratives. Her work does not analyze history's ghosts to exorcise them and restore cohesion in the form of an objective or causal, linear historical narrative. De Zavala includes the temporally disjointed discourses of ghosts in her archive and in doing so creates a new politics of time. The "commerce-without-commerce of ghosts" that Derrida (1994, xviii) describes in *Specters of Marx* appears in De Zavala's work as dialogic relationships across time, facilitated by her assemblage of material relics, buildings, and documents along with ghosts, legends, and apparitions.

Adina De Zavala did not create a single, unitary archive but instead organized multiple archives—archives within archives—that point to one another and outward toward other archives. For example, the buildings she preserved were each archives in their own right, edifices that housed government and church records. They are the sites of authority and historicity from which modern archives would emerge. *History and Legends* also has an archival structure in its collection of photographs and historical documents set in dialogue and gesturing outward toward the missions they reference. Ever knowledgeable about the archival process, De Zavala willed her collection of personal writings, newspaper clippings, organizational records, and artifacts to University of the Incarnate Word and the Dolph Briscoe Center for American History. Some of her smaller archival assemblages are contained within these official collections. For example, in one of her more fascinating juxtapositions, she transformed large financial ledgers into scrapbooks of newspaper clippings and architectural drawings.

De Zavala also finished Edmond J. P. Schmitt's (1901) *Copies from the Archives* after his death from tuberculosis. *Copies from the Archives* is a nineteenth-century multivolume collection of facsimiles of Mesoamerican codices, archaeological descriptions, and Spanish colonial accounts that had been previously collected in Kingsborough's *Antiquities of Mexico*. De Zavala wrote in an editorial note, "[Schmitt's] proof being in many places meaningless, I had to review the entire work and in some places re-write" (Schmitt 1901, 5). Her work on *Copies from the Archives* shows that her interest in archives extended well beyond U.S. national archival constructions. In an address to the Club Women of Texas, titled "Texas History: Written and Unwritten," she said, "In the libraries and archives of Mexico and in the Libraries of Europe are rare and wonderful books and unprinted manuscripts relating to Texas" (n.d.c, 1). The interconnection and multiplicity of archives De Zavala created and referenced reveal the impossibility of repaying a debt to any ghost of the past. Instead of tracing a linear trajectory of debt, her work maps out complex networks of dialogism among the ghosts of the Alamo, the ghosts of other Spanish missions, the ghosts of indigenous peoples, the ghosts of scholars, and, ultimately, her own ghost.

The Adina De Zavala Papers housed at the Dolph Briscoe Center for American History and the University of the Incarnate Word certainly establish De Zavala as a ghost of the archive, but something more fundamental also spectralizes her. By engaging with ghosts to create a dialogic relationship across time and among people, places, and texts, she performs what Avery Gordon has described as "making common cause" with her subject of study. Gordon writes, "Following the ghosts is about making a contact that changes you and refashions the social relations in which you are located. It is about putting life back in where only a vague memory or a bare trace was visible to those who bothered to look. It is sometimes about writing ghost stories, stories that not only repair representational mistakes, but also strive to understand the conditions under which a memory was produced in the first place, toward a countermemory, for the future" (2008, 45). By engaging with ghosts and recognizing her responsibility to them, De Zavala becomes a specter herself—one that can comment, anachronistically, on her own literary recovery. She is a fragmented, absent presence not because of ethnic repression but because she places herself in multiple relations to ghosts of the past and future, ghosts that are, themselves, already disjointed and moving in multiple directions. Srinivas Aravamudan argues that the historian-subject of anachronism is a "fragmented, fragmentary subject, the object, abject, or even reject of historicism, its craven remainder, and indeed an anachronism, but also its pretext, purpose and incitation" (2001, 352). The excess remainder of historicism subverts debt-based economies because there is always something left over—left out—in the reckoning of historical debts. Adina De Zavala can never repay her debt to the ghosts of the past because there will always be another ghost pointing in a different direction and tracing another path of responsibility. Instead of trying to exorcise the ghost by canceling her debt to it, she calls out to the ghosts of San Antonio's past, invites them into her texts and into her archives, and thus becomes disjointed and spectralized in her common cause with them.

De Zavala's writing works against the abstraction of historical meaning that makes ethnic reification possible in South Texas, even if the content of her writing often focuses on Anglo Texans. Indeed, the inclusion alone of Spanish and Mexican ghosts does not safeguard against U.S. enthonationalist reification that produces the United States as inheritor of global colonial modernity. Jesse Alemán analyzes the spectral underpinnings of Manifest Destiny through his concept of a gothic "In-ter" Americanism, which "understands that the nations of the Western hemisphere already contain *within* ('intra') their borders national others whose formative presence is subsequently buried (interred) but nonetheless felt and often expressed through gothic discourse" (2006, 409–10). Inter-American gothic discourse emerges from the repression of the United States' "inter-national" others for the sake of a coherent national identity at the expense of historical and social complexity. The resultant return of the repressed in the form of alienating and alienated gothic specters signals the nation's unpaid debts to the past.

While De Zavala's book does contain some hauntings (namely the ghosts of the Alamo who threaten anyone who tries to demolish the building), her specters just as frequently bequeath gifts, impart knowledge, and dialogically debate Texas history. As Flores asserts, "Adina De Zavala was a patriot of Texas, unabashedly so," but the shape of her Texas nationalism is different from the white supremacist Texas nationalism that dominated the twentieth century (1996, vi). In fact, De Zavala's particular archival iteration of Texas nationalism was a way of navigating U.S. nationalism and its racial ideologies through a multivalent, transnational understanding of Texas history. In a speech celebrating the 107th anniversary of Texas independence, she told audience members, "The Texas Revolution was not a warfare between Americans and Mexicans in Texas. Rather, it was a common fight of Americans and Mexicans against a monster whose greed for power was the spirit of all little men," adding "since Mexico in a very deep sense is the mother country of Texas, our devotion to the cause of liberty would be incomplete if we did not pause to pay tribute to Father Hidalgo" (1943, 2). De Zavala's Texas nationalism is capacious in its incorporation of founding specters.

Perhaps the most complex spectral founder of Texas is Mary Coronel de Agreda. This foremother of Texas is first introduced in *History and Legends'* historical section about Mission San Francisco de los Tejas. According to De Zavala, Mary Coronel de Agreda's desire to convert the Tejas Indians prompted the Spanish colonization of east Texas: "It was the pleading of Mary Coronel de Agreda that had moved [Damían] Manzanet to . . . induce a third expedition that he might accompany it and sooner reach the Tejas Indians" (1996, 66). De Zavala then quotes Manzanet at length, concluding with his account of the Tejas leader's request for blue cloth to make a burial shroud because "in times past they had been visited frequently by a very beautiful woman who used to come down from the hills dressed in blue garments," and he wanted to emulate her. Manzanet concludes that this woman is María Jesús de Agreda, "who was very frequently in those regions" (77). In another section specifically about Mary Coronel de Agreda, De Zavala describes her desire to travel to New Spain "like the men" to convert indigenous peoples: "At last it seemed to her that a way was opened to her to visit the New World, and after a long sea voyage and tedious overland route, she found herself among certain tribes of Indians heretofore unheard of in the Old World" (100). De Zavala then retells the story of Manzanet, the Tejas leader, and the blue cloth. Only toward the end of the biography does De Zavala explain that Mary Coronel de Agreda never physically left Spain but instead experienced visions of the Americas and the Tejas Indians, in which she "visited them in ecstasy" (101).

While other specters are placed clearly in the legends section of *History and Legends*, Mary Coronel de Agreda appears in the history section—in the material world. De Zavala cites Mary Coronel de Agreda's own writing, which is "extant" and "preserved in Fordham College, New York," placing her in the material and intellectual realm of textual production alongside Damían Manzanet, William Barrett Travis, and De Zavala's own writing (1996, 102). In De Zavala's work Mary Coronel de Agreda's embodiment of present absence or dual presence on two continents is not a metaphor, a communal folktale, or an allegory of restoration; it is a historical fact. Mary Coronel de Agreda's bilocation is a doubling of the self, but not in the sense of the

Freudian uncanny double that is a harbinger of death and a loss of wholeness. Her spiritual ecstasy creates a multiplication of the self into a transnational subject that defies the constraints of time and space. There are numerous women that call to mind Mary Coronel de Agreda in *History and Legends*. "The Mysterious Woman in Blue," who lives in the underground passages of San Antonio and bequeaths "the clear-eyed vision of a Joan of Arc" to one woman each generation, is reminiscent of Mary Coronel de Agreda and her blue robes (57). The woman who receives the padre's gift is likewise a figure with special knowledge and a unique connection to San Antonio. These women are not a return of the repressed but a proliferation of archival specters.

To invoke Gordon again, by learning to live with ghosts, De Zavala makes a common cause with Texas specters, striving "to go beyond the fundamental alienation of turning social relations into just the things we know and toward our own reckoning with how we are in these stories" (2008, 118). By inserting herself into the archive and into relationships with specters of the archive, De Zavala opens herself to a new subjectivity outside the linear time of debt and restitution. One possibility is to imagine the specter as mystical or even ordinary rather than gothic. Making a common cause with ghosts is a stylistic and methodological practice of De Zavala's archive formation that scholars can draw on today as they place texts in conversation with one another, looking to recovered authors as interlocutors that shape theory and criticism rather than as objects of analysis. Texas's transnational specters come together in De Zavala's collation of historical material, not as a restoration but as a gift to the future, which implicates the recipient in a dialogue of inheritance.

CHAPTER 4

Modernity and Historical Desire

Differential Time Consciousness in *Caballero*

The early twentieth-century folklorist Jovita González inherited Adina De Zavala's legacy in a number of ways. José Limón, one of the first scholars to discuss González in his seminal work, *Dancing with the Devil*, invites his reader to imagine the 1927 meeting of the Texas Folklore Society, the first one that González attended, upon the encouragement of J. Frank Dobie, her mentor. Dobie was a master of cultural appropriation, as Limón aptly puts it, and his pastoral accounts of lower-class Mexican Texan culture are filled with the condescending tone of imperialist nostalgia. Commenting on González's presentation, Limón asks,

> In Southern Texas in 1927, the war continues . . . but here, at this academic meeting, do not her delightfully accented words flow like soothing balm to the gathered company of mostly white men—some of them rich, powerful men? In his customary cowboy boots, his Stetson hat politely on his lap, does her Don Pancho [J. Frank Dobie] sit there also, probably in the first row? Dare we hope that as she read her paper, she at least *thought* to herself of the "fatalistic" Catarino Garza who shot it out with Captain Bourke? . . . We dare hope, but it is only a hope. (1994, 64–65)

Jovita González would go on to become vice president of the Texas Folklore Society in 1929 and president in 1930 and 1931, again with the support of Dobie. But in 1927 the vice president of the Texas Folklore Society was none other than Adina De Zavala, who, consequently, also had the responsibility of chairing the annual meeting. De Zavala was a charter member of the Texas Folklore Society, as was González's beloved Spanish teacher, Lilia Casis, both of whom helped found the society in 1909, long before Dobie joined.

Limón (1994) charts the development of a contestatory, albeit very sub-dued, rhetoric of ethnic consciousness in González's folklore studies up to her 1935 publication of "The Bullet Swallower" in Dobie's edited folklore collection. But I want to return to the 1927 meeting for a moment. Both De Zavala and González presented on Saturday, De Zavala reading "How the Huisache Came to Bloom" in the afternoon and González reading "Lore of the Texas Vaquero" in the evening. Did they attend each other's presentations? Did they sit near each other during Dobie's opening address the previous evening? Was Lilia Casis there to introduce the women, or had she already done so? The answers to these questions are no clearer than the answers to Limón's questions, but they trace a different set of relationships and a different intellectual inheritance for González. It is an inheritance that repeats itself in the recovery of González's work, when Limón argues, "The problematic with González is not ambivalence but *repression*" (1994, 70; italics added). This time González supposedly sublimates her ethnic consciousness onto a masculine border hero rather than an idealized Spanish past. In Limón's defense he and his own mentee, María Cotera, had yet to discover, or recover, much of González's literary and scholarly work when he wrote *Dancing with the Devil*, but the repetition is uncanny.

Recovery efforts of the 1990s and 2000s would reveal that Jovita González was a renaissance woman of Mexican American letters. In addition to collecting Texas folklore, she wrote an innovative ethnographic history master's thesis that was later used as source material for David Montejano's foundational work *Anglos and Mexicans in the Making of Texas History, 1836–1986* (1987), among others. She also wrote the novel *Dew on the Thorn* (1997), a narrative frame that weaves together folktales and ethnographic descriptions of life in South Texas through the fictional Olivares family, and she coauthored the historical novel *Caballero*, with Margaret Eimer (pen name Eve Raleigh). After she married Edmundo Mireles, González taught English, Spanish, and history classes and coauthored Spanish-language textbooks with Edmundo. González's writing across genres—folklore, history, and fiction—engages with the temporal colonization of South Texas by U.S. modernity as a disruption of Tejana/o tradition. At the same time she poses a feminist critique of Tejano patriarchy. Like María Amparo Ruiz de Burton, González brings multiple forms of time together to deconstruct the temporal ideology of each.

As in *The Squatter and the Don*, temporal colonization in South Texas was the result of U.S. immigrant farmers taking over land previously used for ranching by Tejanas/os, the arrival of the railroad and other commercial and technological developments, and an influx of Anglo-Americans who disrupted preexisting Anglo-Tejano relations by classifying all Tejanos as lower-class Mexicans. These processes occurred several decades later for South Texas than they did for California, in part because the railroad made its way to Brownsville in 1904, whereas the California system extended even to San Diego by 1885. The concomitant material changes in timekeeping—an increased use of wage labor and the coordination of farming practices with railroad schedules and other industrial systems—disrupted long-standing forms of time in South Texas, which had been regulated by patriarchal structures of the Catholic Church and the Tejano ranch.

Jovita González's 1929 history master's thesis, republished in 2006 as *Life along the Border*, documents these changes in a chronological account that includes data from government records, references to secondary sources, and archival research in the United States and Mexico. It also incorporates information from local interviews, personal family records, and firsthand cultural knowledge. The narrative form of her thesis aligns with contemporary U.S. modernist history like that of Walter Prescott Webb or Eugene Barker, her thesis adviser. But its content is markedly different, focusing on the experiences, culture, and ideas of Tejanas/os drawn from their own words. These communal voices make it akin to De Zavala's *History and Legends*, despite González's more direct and processual narrative form. María Cotera, who recovered González's master's thesis, tells readers that Barker was initially reluctant to approve the project because it "lacked sufficient historical references" (2006, 17). For Barker, González's living Tejana/o sources were not legitimate historical references. Their memories did not count the way that other (European and Anglo-American) first-person testimony had long been used in the historical record. Barker was persuaded to approve the project by Carlos Castañeda, the curator of University of Texas's Latin American archival collections, who told him "González's thesis would be used as source material for years to come" (31). Like De Zavala, Jovita González creates history that is a dialogue between past and present, disjoining U.S. narratives of historical development even as she composes an orderly narrative of South Texas's past.

Jovita González ends her thesis with an account of the temporal rupture that U.S. modernity has created for Mexican Americans. She writes of an emerging group of American-educated Texas Mexicans: "Behind them lies a store of traditions of another race, customs of past ages, an innate and inherited love and reverence for another country. Ahead of them lies a struggle of which they are to be the champions. It is a struggle for equality and justice before the law" (2006, 116). Her comment appears to repeat the trope that places Mexican American tradition in the past and U.S. modernity in the present and future, but the future she depicts is not the triumph of U.S. progress but the triumph of Texas Mexicans. Standing at the nexus of disjointed colonial forms of time, young Texas Mexicans link Tejana/o tradition to the future just as González links communal Tejana/o voices with the project of modern historicism. Her master's thesis is not the only text she wrote that places communal dialogue at the juncture of tradition and modernity. González's folklore drew on communal narratives—stories told among groups of Tejanas/os—that she revised into modernist literary form. She had learned this technique from her mentor Dobie, but whereas Dobie's interpretation of Tejana/o folklore rendered it "ahistorical" and "apolitical," González's folklore writing was "artistically implicated in a running political commentary on ethnic, gender and class relations" (Cotera 2006, 13; Limón 1996, xxi). Working in a field that specifically aligned ethnic others with the past through discourses of memory and nostalgia, González used the folklore of her memories and the memories of other Tejanas/os to critique Anglo Texan paradigms of race and history.[1]

González's thesis charts the temporal rupture of U.S. colonization in South

Texas, and her folklore presents a running critique of U.S. modernity, but her coauthored novel, *Caballero*, mines the rupture of tradition and modernity for alternative forms of time from which women and peons can navigate the new structures of domination. *Caballero* is a dialogic rendering of history born of the collaboration between González and Eimer. Cotera calls the novel a "dialogic artifact" built within the politics of coauthorship that "offers a complex feminist critique of the discursive limitation of *both* Mexican and Anglo versions of history" (2008, 201, 203). This critique operates within what I call differential time consciousness, where the narrative shifts between different forms of time to disrupt colonial ideologies of dominance. In González's history, folklore, and fiction writing, the linear progress of U.S. modernity intersects the circular but no less linear time of Tejano tradition. The result is not a *dialectic* resolution that progresses through time but a *dialogic* opening into the future and the past. *Caballero*'s novelistic form and dialogic coauthorship unsettle racialized forms of time and decenter author(ity) as inter- and intracultural dialogue reverberate across the text.

When González and Eimer introduce the novel's protagonists, the Mendoza y Soría family, they also introduce readers to traditional Tejana/o forms of time and the temporal rupture caused by U.S. invasions. Don Santiago is about to lead "El Alabado," a Catholic song of praise, as the sun sets. The interweaving of natural and spiritual time is reminiscent of Eulalia Pérez's account of life at the San Gabriel mission, and Don Santiago's despotic control of time is also a reminder of the mission system's patriarchal subjugation of indigenous peoples. Santiago leads the song, setting the tempo of the rancho, and orders the household "to wait until the last thread of sound [from the hacienda's bell] was scattered before [forming] the vespers assembly, so the master could have these heart filling moments alone" (1996, 3). As patriarch, Santiago controls the time of the hacienda and hoards the best time, the "heart filling moments," to himself. His gendered response to delay reinforces the hacienda's traditional power structures. When his sons, Alvaro and Luis Gonzaga, are late, Santiago thinks, "In spite of his daily admonitions these sons of his failed to be on time. But then, he secretly smiled, they would not be his if they had shown no defiance to the rule." In contrast, Santiago's widowed sister also tarries, "to aggravate him, he knew, because yesterday she had come sooner than he wished and he had told her so" (5). When Don Santiago sings the words of "El Alabado," he feels a "kinship with God" (6). He controls the rhythm of the hacienda, as his wife, sister, children, vaqueros, and peons all respond in unison to his chant. But hoofbeats and the arrival of Santiago's neighbor, Don Gabriel, interrupt his hymn. Gabriel tells him that Texas has joined the union, and they are now all Americanos. Unlike Don Alamar in the *Squatter and the Don*, Don Santiago does not try to accommodate the invaders. He manages to keep his land, but he loses his sense of time, particularly his ability to control time through the repetition of tradition, as signified by the disruption of "El Alabado."

Much of the initial analysis concerning *Caballero* centered on the novel's supposedly dual or divided subject matter. Set during the U.S.-Mexico War, it details the tragic decline of Don Santiago and the romances of his family members. His youngest and most beloved daughter, Susanita, marries a U.S. Army officer from Virginia; her older, religiously devout sister, María de los Angeles, marries a rising Anglo-American politician; and their youngest brother, Luis Gonzaga, leaves Texas with his artistic mentor and confidant, who is also an army officer. Like many historical romances, *Caballero* blends the social and historical context of its setting with that of its composition. The 1996 recovery of *Caballero* was framed, literally, by a kind of dialectic debate about how the text fit into Chicana/o literary history. The coauthored novel was also co-recovered by Limón and Cotera. Limón wrote the foreword for the novel, which places González alongside Américo Paredes, "the primary scholar of Mexican-American South Texas," and subordinates her writing to his as a "kind of precursory text" for Paredes's novel *George Washington Gomez*, also written in the late 1930s (1996, xv).[2] Cotera wrote a critical epilogue for the recovered novel, arguing that if *Caballero* is placed "in the context of other works by women of color and Jovita González de Mireles as a precursor not to Américo Paredes, but to writers like Ana Castillo, Cherríe Moraga and Gloria Anzaldúa, the novel's trenchant critique of the patriarchal world view of foundational texts like [Paredes's] '*With His Pistol in His Hand*' becomes clear" (1996, 340). This recovery framework was the foundation for later debates about *Caballero*'s place in Chicana/o letters and its status as a contestatory (or assimilationist) novel. The many doubles of *Caballero*—the double time of its setting and composition, its double focus of tragic decline and romantic ascendance, its dual authorship and dual recovery—led to critical analysis that focused on dialectic resolutions of the novel's dualisms into a unified meaning. But *Caballero*'s dualisms are a staging ground for multiplicity, not unity.

Moving Differentially across Tradition and Modernity

At first glance *Caballero* depicts the integration of María de los Angeles, Susanita, Luis Gonzaga, and the peons into U.S. modernity through their romantic pairings and economic choices while traditional forms of time unravel with the decline of Don Santiago and his oldest son, Alvaro. The tension between tradition and progress and the seeming supremacy of Anglo-American progress appears in a conversation later in the novel between Don Santiago and Don Gabriel, who says, "It is amazing, Santiago, how their minds leap ahead. It is a quality we lack, for we live in the past and the present and see the future with our emotions only. We believe a thing must be so, or so, and then we wait for it to be so. These *Americanos* say, 'This should be so, I will make it be.' And in that . . . we are already beaten" (González and Eimer 1996, 189). Yet the fact that this conversation takes place between two older rancheros signals its position as the ideological background of *Caballero*, a background across which other discourses of time move throughout the novel.

Narrative interjections and the characters' conflicting relationships with the past and future destabilize constructions of unified, continuous time for either tradition or modernity. Already in the opening scene, Doña Dolores was ruffling Santiago's control of time as she arrived early and then late in retaliation for his rebuke, and after Santiago stops singing "El Alabado" to talk to Gabriel, an elderly servant, Paz, leads the rest of the praise in his stead (and thus structurally replaces the don with an alternate form of authority). The stability of tradition breaks down in the course of the novel's romantic plot, as Don Santiago slowly loses his ability to control the actions of his children and his servants. He can no longer dictate the rhythm and tempo of their lives, and thus for Santiago the harmony of Tejano life falls apart. However, it is simplistic to imagine that Tejano tradition is replaced by U.S. progress in a celebratory narrative of accommodation and assimilation. Within *Caballero* the narrative of progress also collapses through the novel's exposition of South Texas' postwar future. González and Eimer present the linear trajectories of both tradition and progress as always-already internally discontinuous.

The opposition between tradition and modernity appears as the novel's dominant narrative thread when Don Santiago's children leave him to partner with Anglo-American invaders, but tradition and modernity are actually two similar colonial forms of time across which women and lower-class Tejanas/os must move to survive and critique domination. Their movement is differential, to use Chela Sandoval's theorization. For Sandoval, differential consciousness "is a mobile, flexible, diasporic force that migrates between contending ideological systems. . . . It operates as does a technology—a weapon of consciousness that functions like a compass. . . . The effectivity of this cultural mapping depends on its practitioner's continuing and transformative relationship to the social totality. Readings of this shifting totality will determine the interventions—the tactics, ideologies, and discourses that the practitioner chooses in order to pursue a greater good, beginning with the citizen-subject's own survival. Reading signs to determine power relations is its principal technique" (2000, 30). Though Sandoval (2000) describes differential consciousness through the spatial metaphor of cognitive mapping, *Caballero* demonstrates that ideological structures of domination are grounded in specific temporal forms. Despite its shifting nature, the "social totality" that Sandoval describes depends explicitly on modernity's totalization of time—the idea that history is a closed, finite system. The temporal rupture in South Texas is a function of competing colonial systems, where two different totalizations of time collide. *Caballero's* disruptive treatment of time, which refuses synthesis, is a feature of its differential movement across competing ideological forms of time. The result is not a unified position produced through dialectic resolution but a multiplicity of coexisting temporalities that subjects can inhabit and deploy as strategies for survival amid shifting systems of domination.

Dialogism is not a feature of Sandoval's theory, but it is the medium through which differential consciousness operates. Both María Cotera and J. Javier Rodríguez describe *Caballero* as dialogic in their move away from earlier dualistic and dialectic analyses. Rodríguez draws on the Bakhtinain tradition of novelistic polyvocality, writing, "The dialogism of novels can be seen as already antagonistic to the singular law of the patriarch" (2008, 126). For Cotera the dialogue of coauthorship deconstructs the unitary nature of author(ity), replacing it with multiplicity and an in-between space of narrative negotiation because it denies a "stable ideological center to the narrative, and thus present[s] a meta-textual challenge to the autonomous subject-in-resistance upon which Don Santiago grounds his oppositional logic" (2008, 215). *Caballero* offers an opportunity for exploring what dialogic form does—it disrupts authority—but more important, it offers an opportunity to understand *how* dialogism works as a disruptive force. Dialogism is a temporal methodology capable of posing an alternative to modernity's underlying temporality of linear, empty, homogenous time.

Mikhail Bakhtin wrote against dialectic synthesis as he developed the concept of dialogism in his theory of the novel. Dialogue is a perpetual interaction, constantly coalescing and recoalescing to create new social potentials in an open, unfinalizable form. The openness that dialogue demands undermines any totalizing or linear conception of history. For Bakhtin, "Dialectics abstracts the dialogic from dialogue. It finalizes and systematizes dialogue. Individual agency, particular evaluations, the rootedness in the word that creates real potential for the unforeseen are reified and die" (Morson and Emerson 1990, 57). When a conversation is teleological and systematic (think the Platonic dialogues), it becomes dialectic and is no longer part of what Bakhtin calls dialogic. As Cotera (2008) and Rodríguez (2008) argue, the dialogic imagination undermines singular subjectivity like that enacted by Don Santiago. They explain that dialogic multiplicity disrupts the unity, autonomy, and authority of Don Santiago's patriarchal self. What makes this possible, though, is the unfinalizability of dialogue—its temporal incompleteness.

Temporality operates through language as a function of syntax and narrative. The constant dialogue of internal (psychological) and intersubjective (social) existence interanimates diverse forms of time. Indeed, Bakhtin's essay "Forms of Time and the Chronotope in the Novel" accounts for the way time works dialogically in novels. A chronotope is the solidification of time and space in a novel, where time remains the primary category. He writes, "Chronotopes are mutually inclusive, they co-exist, they may be interwoven with, replace or oppose one another, contradict or find themselves in ever more complex interrelationships. The relationships themselves that exist *among* chronotopes cannot exist *within* chronotopes. The general characteristic of these interactions is that they are *dialogical*" (1981, 252). Gary Saul Morson and Caryl Emerson explain that dialogic discourses do not renounce their "out-sideness" to one another in an act of synthesis but rather draw on their differences as a "surplus of vision" so that each sheds light on the other (1990, 54).

Bakhtin's (1981) interanimation of discourses is relevant to Sandoval's (2000) differential consciousness and other decolonial Chicana feminist theories. Dialogism is what makes it possible to view multiple ideological formations from different vantage points and also what makes it necessary to deploy oppositional modes of consciousness differentially rather than synthesize them into a singular, unified form of opposition. Unified opposition to a totalized system of oppression can only result in the synthesis of a new totality through a dialectic process. The pitfalls of dialectic contestation is, in fact, one of Chicana feminism's primary critiques of Chicano nationalism and Anglo-American feminism. Gloria Anzaldúa writes of the new mestiza consciousness, "It is not enough to stand on the opposite river bank shouting questions, challenging patriarchal white conventions. . . . All reaction is limited by, and dependent upon, what it is reacting against" (1987, 100). This is the problem with the linear trajectory of dialectic interpretation and, in particular, with the conception of history as a dialectic unfolding through linear time. Differential consciousness is a dialogic and therefore temporal practice. Morson and Emerson write, "We think of individual selves occupying a specific place at a specific time. But although that is true of and necessary for physical bodies, it is untrue of psyches or of any other cultural entities" (1990, 54, 51). Dialogic formations—and the social and psychic subjects they interanimate—always inhabit more than one form of time.

For true critique and difference to occur, nonreified, nonlinear movement across (ideological) discourses must remain temporally open rather than mapped out and processual. While movement across borders has been privileged as a key feature of Chicana/o subjectivity, the ability to inhabit multiple spaces and identities at once is a temporal act. Emma Pérez recognizes this when she writes that the interstitial gaps in history's discursive formations "interrupt the linear model of time, and it is in such locations that oppositional, subaltern histories can be found" (1999, 120). She identifies movement within these interstitial gaps with Sandoval's methodology of differential consciousness (5). The interstitial spaces in linear history are precisely what Pérez terms "third space feminism." But the fact that these interstices are outside of linear time does not mean they aren't *of time*; they are, in fact, alternative forms of time. Third-space feminism could just as likely be called third-time feminism. *Caballero*'s movement between U.S. modernity and Tejano tradition, using the discourse of each to deconstruct the other, is the temporal embodiment of both differential consciousness and third-space feminism.

Caballero disrupts Tejano tradition and U.S. modernity by placing their forms of time in dialogic relation. Though tradition and modernity may seem to present opposing temporalities, they share some key features, particularly in the power structures and hegemony that they create. The logic of tradition is that of repetition, in which the present draws meaning from its relation to the past and is valued according to its ability to create continuity between past and future. The circularity of tradition is also its linearity, because deviation from the trajectory of return is considered a transgression, much like the Mendoza y Soría daughters' refusal to participate in traditional Tejana/o marriages sanctioned by their father. In contrast, U.S. modernity's ideology of progress is a straight line that moves toward an imagined future, which is different from and, supposedly, better than the past. Yet the line of progress is also a form of continuity between past, present, and future. The continuity of progress appears when the *new* is a transmutation of the old (like scientific discourses of race and gender that justify long-standing social hierarchies) or when present is projected onto past (like Manifest Destiny's depiction of the present hegemony as always-already inevitable). Lee Bebout, focusing on *Caballero*'s two systems of heteropatriarchal dominance, writes, "Whether through the semi-feudal hacienda system of Spain and Mexico or through the 'Enlightened' wage-labor capitalism of the United States, both models are concerned with securing and maintaining racial and economic power in the future" (2015, 358). Tejano tradition and U.S. modernity secure their hegemony through linear and, to varying degrees, recursive temporal structures that take different shapes but function similarly.

Caballero subverts the temporality of Tejano tradition by locating modernity, not in the Americano's arrival but in the very foundation of Don Santiago's heritage. The novel's foreword depicts Rancho La Palma's founding in 1748. Don Santiago's grandfather, Don José Ramón, stands on a "bluff that looked like the fragment of a great wall" above Rancho La Palma and surveys the land (González and Eimer 1996, xxxvi). The bluff works to frame the narrative as the locale of the first and last scene and is a place to which Don Santiago returns throughout the novel. It marks the cyclical continuity of Tejano tradition. The bluff connects Santiago to the past through a lineage of inheritance and patriarchal dominance that constructs his own identity in the 1840s present of the novel. The view from the bluff reinforces the hegemony of patriarchal tradition. As Monika Kaup writes, "The Don appropriates the land by imposing a single, fixed perspective. Following the post-Renaissance landscape convention, where the perspective becomes 'truth itself,' Don Santiago asserts sole ownership, excluding social relationships other than his own and rendering invisible domestic labor via aesthetic objectification" (2005, 570). The materiality of the land that Santiago looks at and stands on reinforces his patriarchal identity as the real and natural relation to a continuous system of meaning handed down from his forbearers. The constancy of the natural landscape and its cyclical, seasonal changes reinforce traditional forms of time.

Embedded in this seeming continuity, however, is a rupture from the past at the moment of Rancho La Palma's foundation. Don José Ramón builds his hacienda on the 1748 Tejas frontier so that he can "rear his family and keep the old ways and traditions safely away from the perfidious influence of Mexico City and the infiltration of foreign doctrines; not only for himself but for the generations to come" (González and Eimer 1996, xxxvi). The Mexican identity that Don Santiago clings to throughout the novel is thus the very identity that Don José Ramón is trying to escape. The heart of Mexico is already "foreign" on the first page of the foreword, and indeed, it is also modern in the sense that Don José Ramón is likely referring to Bourbon reforms and the resultant European Enlightenment ideas that begun impacting Mexico in the eighteenth century. Raúl Coronado places these changes at the heart of a distinctly Hispanophone formation of modernity in eighteenth- and early nineteenth-century Texas in *A World Not to Come*.[3] Coronado's analytic history of ideas and textual production in Texas eloquently describes some of the temporal collisions that appear in *Caballero*, despite the different historical periods covered by the novel and his monograph. These include competing ideas of sovereignty and social cohesion within a Catholic epistemology. Though *Caballero* situates the U.S.-Mexico War as the primary moment of temporal disruption, it embeds a trace of Tejana/o and Mexican modernity in the narrative's prehistory. Rancho La Palma's origin is as much a rupture of modernity as it is a continuation of tradition.

While *Caballero* undermines the continuity of tradition at the moment of Rancho La Palma's foundation, its critique of Anglo-American progress is set in the liminal futurity of Manifest Destiny. The chiasmic interplay of Don Santiago's tragic decline and his daughters' increasing agency during the U.S.-Mexico War fills the space of the plot, but Texas's postwar future also makes its way into the novel through narrative digressions into the future anterior. The future anterior is the temporal gap between the time of a narrative's setting and the time of its composition or, grammatically speaking, *what will have happened*. The future anterior structures both novelistic form—a completed narrative experienced through the linear process of reading—and the supposedly postmodern act of experiencing the present as the future's past, when a newsworthy current event is described as a "historic moment" or when daily activities are referred to as "making memories." Fredric Jameson describes the effect of the future anterior in literature as "the estrangement and renewal as history of our own reading present" (1991, 285). But within the genre of historical fiction, where readers already know *what will have happened*, the effect is reversed, and the future anterior is an estrangement and renewal of history as our reading present. Jameson's future anterior transforms the present into a kind of history yet to be historicized, but historical fiction transforms history into a reading present with the potential to be historicized in new ways. The future anterior is thus a strategic space for critiquing the temporal ideology of Manifest Destiny. As I discussed in chapter 1, nineteenth-century Manifest Destiny constructed the future as having already happened by projecting U.S. domination of the present onto a future of perpetual growth and expansion and foreclosing all other historical possibilities. *Caballero*'s narrative interjections into the future anterior unravel the temporal ideology of Manifest

Destiny by reopening the past to the phenomenology and hermeneutics of the reading present.

In *Caballero* two narrative digressions forecast the devastation that would come to Texas after the end of the U.S.-Mexico War. When Don Santiago finds violent squatters on his land, the narrator explains, "It was a scene that was to be repeated in variation for many years to come," and recasts the "pioneer" of U.S. Manifest Destiny as "the fugitive, . . . the land-greedy . . . , the trash, the *'puerco'* . . . the wanderer, fleeing nothing but himself; the adventurer, his conscience and his scruples long dead" (González and Eimer 1996, 194). The second major digression into the future appears in the last chapter, where the authors write, "The War, said Washington, was over. Peace, said Washington, was here. War, Texas knew, is a fecund mother whose children spring from her full grown. Want, wrapped in tattered sheet; . . . Revenge, and Hatred, and Murder, and Greed—ah, Greed!—the four that never slept. The War. Yes, the War was over. So said the record. Texas wrote its history with a scratchy, blotty pen and called its southern line the 'bloody border'" (331). In both instances a revelation of the region's postwar future troubles the dominant Anglo narrative of Texas history. These comments open Texas's future anterior into a perpetual repetition of violence that counters Manifest Destiny's narrative of closure. While Manifest Destiny figures conquest as always-already complete (even when it has yet to be enacted), *Caballero* narrates conquest as a perpetual process of violence, structurally incapable of achieving resolution.

John Morán González contextualizes *Caballero* within an important resurgence of Manifest Destiny, the 1930s centennial discourse that celebrated the hundredth anniversary of Texas independence. He explains, "Centennial discourses . . . celebrated the U.S.-Mexico War as the fulfillment of a national Manifest Destiny begun at San Jacinto" (2009, 182). In contrast, *Caballero*'s future anterior presents the war not as the fulfillment but as the failure of Manifest Destiny's promise to spread progress in the form of economic prosperity and democratic inclusion. The Texas centennial's valorization of Manifest Destiny that John Morán González describes also perpetuated Manifest Destiny's colonization and oppression by justifying U.S. colonial practices in the present. The Texas centennial was a moment of U.S. modernity's hegemonic self-justification through public history, projecting current

(1930s) power structures onto both past and future. *Caballero's* future anterior reopens the past (as the novel's future) to critique the 1930s present created by U.S. domination. *Caballero's* dialogic forms of time disrupt not only Tejana/o nostalgia for the prewar past but also Anglo Texan nostalgia for a preindustrial frontier of pioneers and cowboys. The entanglement of past, present, and future in totalizing, hegemonic constructions of time allows the novel's critique of any one form of time to reverberate across all the ideological uses of time made by a specific power system.

Social Memory in the Borderland

González and Eimer's dialogic forms of time move beyond tradition and modernity. The differential time consciousness displayed in the novel deconstructs hegemony, yes, but it also makes space for other forms of time and other ways of relating to the past and the future. One key method of critique within the novel is memory. *Caballero* moves differentially across time through various characters' acts of remembering. Memories create intersubjective dialogues as they move between personal and social formations of the past. Though shaped by shared events and shared narrations, memories draw on an individual's unique subject position and experiences. Memories act as responsive, mobile relationships to the past rather than reified, linear narratives of events ordered by cause and effect.

It is important to distinguish between mobile, intersubjective, dialogic memories and what has been called cultural or collective memory, which is the kind of memorialization visible in the modern Alamo building. Vincent Pérez (2004) and Richard Flores (1998) discuss cultural memory at length in relation to the hacienda and the Alamo, respectively. Pérez writes that even countercultural memories can "cement layers of history and memory together in an iconic monument to the past, burying contrary memories in their project to buttress Mexican-American ethnic identity" (2004, 475). Flores and Pérez both draw on the work of Pierre Nora (1989) to discuss the socially charged symbols of cultural memory. Nora theorizes cultural memory as a counter to modernist history. But it actually works more like a supplement to modern history that draws heavily on historical time in its production of cultural consolidation. Nora's classic theorization of memory sites—material objects of cultural memory—posits that traditional memory has become unmoored in the wake of modernity. Premodern memory allowed people to experience the present as an organic continuation of the past, akin to Benedict Anderson's assertion that premodern peoples "had no conception of history as an endless chain of cause and effect or of radical separations between past and present" (2006, 23). For Nora history opposes "true memory" because it does not enact a continuation of the past in the present but instead represents the past *to* the present, reinforcing modernity's radical discontinuity with the past (1989, 13). But Nora fails to recognize that both organic premodern memory and modern (cultural nationalist) memory sites are rooted in the racial logic of modern temporality, which, through discourses of ethnography and anthropology, constructs ethnic subjects as natural, illogical, and traditional in opposition to cultured, scientific, and progressive Euro-American subjects. The premodern is thus a creation of, not a predecessor to, modernity. Like tradition and modernity, cultural memory and history are interlinked.

Professional historical discourses and sites of collective memory work together through an interplay of contingent and totalized time when we consider that memory sites act metonymically. The logic of metonymy itself depends on a unified, totalized past; the situated, contingent hacienda projects the wholeness of Mexican American culture that it supposedly stands in for. Only by imagining historical time as complete or totalized can modernity allow memory sites to stand in metonymically for that completeness, that unified identity, which, in fact, was always already an imagined completeness. Modernity's totalization of time through historical discourse is what makes collective memory, channeled through memory sites, possible. The Alamo becomes the totality of history for Anglo Texans only when history is already imagined as totality. Metonymy's projection of totality is the logic that sustained J. Frank Dobie's belief that folklore could capture the spirit of a particular people because the folk culture he envisioned was already a homogenous, totalized ethnological unit before he set pen to paper.

What I am calling "social memory" is quite different from cultural memory. It is an active, intersubjective engagement with the past, and it works specifically against hegemonic cultural memory. Throughout *Caballero* Doña

Dolores's memories are perhaps most disruptive to hegemonic formations of the Tejano past. She repeatedly tries to reform Don Santiago's view of Americanos by reminding him of a past she believes he has forgotten. Yet their differing memories of a shared family history correlate to their different positions within the Tejano patriarchy. Through the lens of Don Santiago's memory, we learn that Santiago and Dolores's brother, Ramón, returned home from the Battle of the Alamo suffering severe internal wounds yet praising his Americano opponents. Not realizing that Ramón was wounded, their father, Don Francisco, struck Ramón for his insolence and thus dealt the deathblow to his own son. Don Santiago's memory focuses on the wounds Ramón received at the Alamo and the "devil's charm and contamination" that caused Ramón to praise his enemies (González and Eimer 1996, 200). Santiago's memory is shaped by Don Francisco's deathbed directive to "remember always that Ramón was killed because he defended his country against them" (19). In an ironic reversal, Francisco is the one who gives an injunction to remember the Alamo foreclosing the intercultural dialogue that Ramón tried to articulate before he died. Though Dolores is never able to reshape Santiago's memories, her constant reminders present an alternate history of patriarchal rule as destructive and tyrannical. Her relationship to the past interanimates Santiago's as she appears even within the frame of his own memory. Dolores is present throughout the scenes of Santiago's memory, and after he recalls his father's anger-filled deathbed command to "fight [Americanos] to the end," he also recalls how Dolores "put her arms around her brother's neck and sobbed: 'Santiago let us never be like that, never!'" (20). Just as De Zavala disrupted the Daughters of the Republic of Texas's construction of the Alamo as a symbol of Anglo-American supremacy, Dolores disrupts Francisco's and Santiago's cultural memories of the Alamo that also constructs it through the binary opposition of Mexican and Anglo Texan.

Dolores's and Santiago's discordant dialogic memory moves well beyond the incident of their brother's death. Like the rupture of modernity at the foundation of Rancho La Palma, Dolores's understanding of heritage and inheritance disrupts the patrilineal hierarchy on which Santiago's unified self-conception depends. In a quarrel about traveling to Matamoros for the winter, Don Santiago tells his sister, "I command your respect if not your obedience. I am master here!" to which Dolores responds, "Go into the *sala* and read what your grandfather carved on the rafter, that the Lord is the master here. His things come first. Why did your grandfather build the house in Matamoros? So we could renew our souls by going to church" (González and Eimer 1996, 26). For Doña Dolores, the family motto, *Dios es Señor de esta casa*, carved in gothic letters on the central beam of the *sala*, does not instill the collective memory of divinely ordained patriarchs who rule in God's stead. She reads in the ancestral inscription an indictment against the arrogance, violence, and oppression perpetrated by patriarchs who fail to submit to God's authority. The act of reminding situates memory as a social experience. It depicts the past as a space of dialogic negotiations rather than a reified totality.

Dolores maintains a multifaceted relation to her *antepasados/as* that contrasts sharply with Santiago's understanding of linear, patriarchal descent. She links her identity not only to her grandfather's inscription but also to a history of female endurance that has existed in the hacienda since the first doña, brought to Rancho La Palma against her will, became its matriarch. Doña Dolores's grandmother, Susana Ulloa, "bore her burden bravely and well," and she alone appreciated the "beauty of soul and intelligence" in her daughter-in-law, Amalia Soría, who was Dolores's, Ramón's, and Santiago's mother (González and Eimer 1996, xxxviii–xxxix). When Amalia dies, Doña Susana nurtures Dolores's independent spirit with the excuse that Dolores's lack of beauty might be compensated by independence, but also with the knowledge that Doña Susana's own beauty had done nothing to protect her from the isolation of the Texas frontier. Susana Ulloa teaches her grandchildren a different sense of traditional continuity: "Religion, traditions, the ways that had survived centuries and received permanence through that survival, gentility—all those Susana inculcated in her grandchildren" (xxxix). Doña Dolores draws on this past in her own memories of family history, and its difference from patriarchal tradition helps her survive the temporal rupture brought by U.S. modernity.

Susana Ulloa likewise bestows a cultural inheritance on Don Santiago when she tells him at her death, "You will someday be master of Rancho La Palma de Cristo. . . . It was your grandfather's dream, which he built into reality. It was my entire life. Santiago, be worthy of Rancho La Palma, and the things for which it stands" (González and Eimer 1996, xxxix). Marissa López points out that "being worthy of the 'things for which [Rancho La Palma] stands' is an ambiguous task." Quite different from Don Francisco's vengeful deathbed exhortation, Doña Susana's injunction "presents the future don with the opposition between the 'dream of a great hacienda' and Susana's exploited life, but the reader is unsure of which Santiago is to be worthy: the abstract dream or the material life, or perhaps she means for him to be worthy of the fact that the two run at cross purposes" (2011, 135). It is precisely the cross purposes that Santiago is unable to navigate. While Dolores moves between the inheritance of her mother, grandmother, father, and grandfather, Santiago cannot incorporate women's sacrifice into his understanding of duty, tradition, or identity. In contrast to Dolores's social memory, Don Santiago constructs a hegemonic cultural memory of the hacienda as an idealized space of social cohesion under his command.

After shamefully whipping Rancho La Palma's elderly goatherd for providing meat to Texas Rangers, Santiago returns to the bluff overlooking Rancho La Palma to find solace in his patriarchal gaze. Instead, he finds a specter of himself, who tries to remind Santiago that the hacienda is a place of communal linkage and that Santiago's inheritance and responsibilities are multiple. The "man with his own face came and stood beside" Santiago, telling him, "Will you in the end know happiness if you deny it to them? . . . Have you forgotten that the master must be servant also? Who is master, the one who lashes, or the one who stays his hand? Learn first to master that most unruly of servants—yourself. . . . You can be the man you are or the one I am. You know me. I am the part given to you by your splendid mother" (González and Eimer 1996, 173). Don Santiago's encounter with his other self, the ghost of himself, is a spectral moment, what Jacques Derrida describes as "a moment that no longer belongs to time, if one understands by this word the linking of modalized presents" (1994, xx). But Santiago cannot exit the linear time of his patriarchal inheritance to acknowledge the multiplicity that his maternal inheritance brings to his past and his identity; he "struck out with empty hand at the man with the quiet eyes, and struck again and again" (González and Eimer 1996, 173). Santiago may be worthy of the "dream of a great hacienda," but the fact that he cannot be worthy of the hacienda's multiple pasts leaves him immobilized amid the shifting ground of colonization that women in his family are better able to navigate (López 2011, 135).

Doña Dolores's matrilineal memories expose fissures within Tejano cultural memory, yet she also reveals the way that social remembering connects people. Though Don Santiago cannot incorporate the history of women's sacrifice into his understanding of the past, *Caballero* indicates that haciendados are not all modeled after Santiago. Few scholars note the novel's fourth romance, between Doña Dolores and Gabriel del Lago, perhaps because it develops late in the novel and late in the lives of the two lovers, but this romance is no less important than those of Santiago's children. Dolores expects men to forget aspects of the past that hold significance for women despite, or perhaps because of, her constant reminders to Santiago. When Susanita is hastily betrothed to Gabriel del Lago to keep her from marrying Warrener, the widowed Dolores gives Susanita her old trousseau and comments on the groom's belt, "Many a tear I wove into this for Anselmo [her deceased spouse]," adding, "If Gabriel recognizes it so much the better, though he won't; man demands that we slave for him and never looks at the finished work" (González and Eimer 1996, 256). After Susanita breaks the engagement, and Gabriel admits to Dolores that he is glad of it, Dolores and Gabriel recognize their own love in an act of shared memory. Gabriel tells her, "I remember when you were married. You looked so forlorn and unhappy I could have wept. I did weep. I felt such grief for you, Dolores" (323).

Unlike Santiago, Gabriel recognizes women's suffering and sacrifice within the tradition of patriarchal dominance. His and Dolores's shared memory does not embody the continuation of a unified Tejana/o cultural tradition. Instead, the older lovers flout the precepts of tradition and marry each other despite their age and despite the disapproval of Don Santiago, the priest marrying them, and, Dolores suspects, many of her female friends. Like the more frequently analyzed romance between Luis Gonzaga and Captain Devlin, Dolores and Gabriel's relationship is nonreproductive. But unlike the novel's queer romance, which Bebout (2015) argues has an unwritten and unimaginable future that defies the temporality of biological reproduction, Dolores and Gabriel's heteronormative romance remains within South Texas, where they will provide an alternate inheritance for Santiago's children and grandchildren. Dolores and Gabriel's relationship disrupts the unified linearity of patriarchal descent, albeit less radically than Luis Gonzaga and Captain Devlin, because their social acts of remembering create a dialogic relation to the past. Indeed, Gabriel del Lago has already offered to give Susanita's baby his mother's rosary if the child is a girl, positing new Tejana linkages beyond the bounds of the Mendoza y Soría family's patriarchal lineage.

Desiring Subjectivity

Caballero is a metahistorical novel that explores the links between professional discourses of history, ethnographic practices (like folklore studies), and cultural memory (like the Texas centennial). Limón (1999), drawing on Doris Sommer (1991), reads *Caballero* as an allegory for Tejana/o integration into U.S. modernity through the romances of Susanita and María de los Angeles. Sommer examines nineteenth-century Latin American romantic novels as allegories of national consolidation. In Sommer's analysis romantic desire becomes a metaphor for history—the way history can or should unfold. But what if *Caballero* presents history as a metaphor for desire, a third-time/ space feminist desire for that which has no place in modernity? Third-space feminism conceives of desire and memory as always historically conditioned. Emma Pérez describes memory as an iteration of desire that is historically inscribed on the body. She writes, "The body constructs its desire through memory, and it constructs its memory through desire. That which may not yet be—but will be—is the scenario created to satisfy desire, where bodies meet as if they had already met" (1999, 109). Instead of desire as the engine of history, historical experience is the condition that shapes desire and the ways that subjects are able to remember. Patriarchal tradition and U.S. history are products of white men's memory and desire, where the sexual politics of colonization shape historical possibility. While the novel's romances may allegorize different potential histories as different kinds of national formations, underlying the romance plot is an interrogation of historical narrative that deconstructs linear time as a function of colonial desire.

John Morán González describes women's desire in the novel as a modernizing force that emphasizes the importance of intersubjective (as opposed to subject and object) relationships. For him González and Eimer present desire and consent as a model for egalitarian cross-cultural relations (2009, 180). The structure of the novel, however, indicates that U.S. modernity and the progress it promises are riddled with hypocrisy. Thus, Anglo-America's promise of egalitarian relationships, be they romantic, political, or economic, become highly suspect in light of *Caballero*'s postwar narrative digressions.[4] The Mendoza y Soría women's desires are constrained by patriarchal and colonial conditions. Their choices cannot be read as the fulfillment of their agency as freely desiring subjects. Marissa López's analysis of women's desire in *Caballero* is more fruitful. She describes a "tension between form and content that can be read as a commentary on the viability of historical narrative" within the novel (2011, 127). Historical narrative is disrupted in part because the "irrationality (in terms of being outside a closed system) of women's desire correlates to the irrationality of history in *Caballero*" (142). Women's desire is "irrational" because the closed system of history corresponds to the closed system of heteropatriarchal colonial desire.

Susanita's and María de los Angeles's romantic pairings are two different iterations of the way that women's desire is inscribed by the colonial time of modernity. López maintains that the women's "rejection of past influence signals a rejection of the racialization of time and knowing," yet the rejection of past values is a constitutive feature of modernity, which privileges the new through a constant negation of the past (2011, 138). Susanita's and Angela's interest in newly arrived Anglo-American suitors rather than traditional Tejano husbands mirrors modernity's privileging of the new (in U.S. modernity, this is always an Anglo-American newness), which is perhaps the primary reason the novel has been read as a call to embrace U.S. modernity. Rather than embracing U.S. modernity, however, the Mendoza y Soría sisters move differentially through modern forms of time in a bid for social agency. Their differential movement is most apparent in María de los Angeles's marriage, which is based on mutual respect and mutual benefit rather than on the true love typically presented in historical romance. Don Santiago forbids his pious daughter from entering the convent, and so María de los Angeles finds an outlet for her desire to do good works in a marriage to Red McLane. She will be able to help her people through access to Red's political clout, and he will gain political influence over Mexican American voters by marrying an upper-class Tejana. Emma Pérez's comment about another Tejana's differential movement could apply to María de los Angeles here: "She is still trapped in the confines of patriarchal conditions—and those are the conditions that condition her—but we cannot forget how she manipulates that control for her own benefit, for her own agency" (1999, 118).[5] María de los Angeles does not embrace modernity but moves within it, using it as a tool to claim her own agency. Denied the limited agency of joining a convent, she chooses the limited agency of an Anglo politician's racialized wife. Angela uses the progressive time of cultural integration to perform her own acts of mercy, which exist in a wholly different temporal construction—one of spiritual redemption.

Susanita's movement within U.S. modernity is more complex. It may be "ahistorical," as López (2011, 138) asserts, but that does not mean it is atemporal. Susanita and Robert Warrener's love is destined and, as the novel describes, eternal. When Alvaro threatens Warrener for dancing with Susanita, Warrener thinks in response, "Why, I have always known Susanita. She is why I left Virginia and home and came here. Don't you see she was waiting for me to come to her" (González and Eimer 1996, 94). Their love is outside the processual time of cause and effect, but as a preordained relationship—a romance of *destiny*—their love is not outside U.S. modernity's forms of time. While María de los Angeles's romance figures the historical process of ethnic integration through linear time, Susanita's eternal romance follows the logic of Manifest Destiny. It is the relationship between Americano and Tejana that has always already existed. The temporalities of Susanita's and Angela's romances work in tandem as two forms of U.S. colonial time: historical progress and Manifest Destiny. Susanita's romance operates in the more abstract form of time because, unlike María de los Angeles, who desires agency, Susanita's desire is for desire itself. She tells her sister, "Do you know, Angela, I often wonder if there isn't a part of us that is completely ours given to us at birth which cannot possibly belong to any one else. How can we completely belong to *papá*, if we have separate souls?" (212). Susanita's decolonial desire is the remembrance of herself *as* desiring subject rather than desired object. Like María de los Angeles, Susanita moves within the conditions of colonization to choose the constraints of Anglo-American paternalism over those of Tejano patriarchy. To call on Emma Pérez again: "Tracking desire historically invokes the site of fantasy where resistance is possible, perhaps even making revolution possible" (1999, 110). History—colonial history—conditions desire, but as differential consciousness moves across ideological forms of time, the movement itself, not the dialogue but the dialogic, opens a third space/time, a desire to desire differently.

Unlike the Mendoza y Soría daughters, the differential movement of peons is largely invisible throughout the novel. The most obvious sign of peons' agency is their gradual disappearance from the hacienda to seek paid employment with Anglo-American ranchers in what Cotera calls their "love affair with free market capitalism" (2008, 200). Manuelito, great-grandson of the Mendoza y Sorías' aged housekeeper, Paz, is the most conspicuous peon in the novel. He moves across cultural formations adroitly. After spending time in Matamoros during the family's winter holiday, Manuelito shows up wearing the coat of a U.S. soldier and the pants of a Texas Ranger. When Santiago threatens to whip him, Manuel taunts the don with a string of English phrases he learned in Bonny's tavern; "he chanted again in the infidel's language: 'Manuel like 'Mericans, like bacon and ham, damn it all. Hurry up, Bony, you old-poke, three of a kind beets two pair, the top o' the morning to ye, holy Saint Michael. Manuel you little devil bring me a drink, this is a helluva hole.' The words came in confusion and highly accented, sounding like wild curses to the ears so new to them" (González and Eimer 1996, 101). Manuel's deployment of U.S. slang is a breakdown of the temporal cohesion that structures language. It is a nonnarrative eruption that, for Don Santiago, threatens the coherence of Tejano society. Manuel's nascent bilingualism signals his ability to cross culture and class boundaries, as he later becomes a messenger for Robert's and Susanita's love notes and eventually learns to read and write in English and joins the U.S. Army. After Manuelito runs away to join the army, he writes his grandmother, Paz a brief letter:

> *Abuelita, estoy bien y muy contento; te quiero mucho* (Grandma, I love you and am well and happy). The "Manuel" was carefully done in even letters, the period after it was very black and round. . . . It was not until she was in bed that she remembered how incensed she had been when Estéban had repeated what the *Americano* with the yellow beard had told him,

that all men were born free and had the right to learn to read and write if they cared to. One was born to be master, another to serve that master in humility, without aspiration. Yet it seemed right that Manuel should be more than an unlettered peon. But if it was right for Manuel it was right for another, and that was not right at all. Round and round went Paz, reasoning until finally exhaustion brought sleep. (205)

Paz's questioning desire is reminiscent of Susanita's desire for subjectivity, but Paz's desired subjectivity is for her grandson, for him to inscribe his own name. The Americano's words are anachronistic for the 1840s, when many states in the South and North had antiliteracy laws, signaling, perhaps, historical excess as much as historical amnesia. The letter, too, signals a surplus of meaning. After Susanita read the letter to Paz, "Tears stood in the old eyes as she rushed away, clasping this miracle to her breast" (González and Eimer 1996, 205). The "miracle" of Manuelito's writing punctures time and brings discord into Paz's epistemology, but it is a discord of love and desire. Manuel is again moving differently through language. He writes in Spanish, using the tools of literacy he learned in the U.S. Army camp to communicate his own love and subjectivity.

Other peons flee from the rancho secretly. González and Eimer are explicit about the sexual threat that haciendados pose to peon women. Gregorio, the arborist and gardener of Rancho La Palma, implores Don Santiago to keep Alvaro away from his granddaughter, but Santiago affirms his son's sexual rights to peon women, telling Gregorio, "The servant belongs to the master. . . . God made the one to serve the other, and that is the law. You know the saying, 'tie up your little hen, for my rooster has a world to roam'" (González and Eimer 1996, 297). Afterward Gregorio; his wife, Anna; and his granddaughter, Juanita, escape to an Anglo ranch just before Alvaro arrives home with plans to rape Juanita. John Alba Cutler explains, "At the point where Don Santiago most harshly asserts the racial difference between himself and the *peons*, Gregorio is shown to be his moral superior" (2015, 49). Here and elsewhere Santiago's flawed understanding of religion underlies his failure to maintain tradition.

In her master's thesis Jovita González is not as explicit, but she writes, "The fact that the peón was economically dependent caused all the evils resulting from this system of peonage" (2006, 77). Her thesis sheds further light on the novel when she writes about the economic transition to wage labor that occurred in the 1920s that she and Eimer anachronistically placed in the novel: "These people are content with their economic uplift and care little or nothing as to the treatment they receive from their American masters. They do not resent any racial distinction or discrimination, the difference between them and their masters is no different than that which separated them from their former *amos*" (1996, 110–11). Here Anglo-Americans are no less opprobrious than Tejano "masters," but González softens her critique of both by referencing vague "discrimination" rather than rape. Her official historical discourse repeats the patronizing language of contentment and apathy used by U.S. and Tejana/o colonizers to describe lower-class Mexican Americans. In this light the peons' differential consciousness exists in the margins of *Caballero*, as they move across different forms of time to become capitalist consumers and mobile laborers, exiting the structural position of debt peonage but remaining in the role of subservient and contented laborers. Like the Mendoza y Soría sisters, the peons' desire is constrained by colonial history—González and Eimer's, if not their own.

The novel also critiques Don Santiago's linear, hierarchical epistemology of authority and continuity by setting it against myriad Catholic forms of time. Thus, religion acts as another locus of differential time consciousness, particularly for characters on the periphery of the plot. Doña María Petronilla enacts prefiguration in her only instance of rebellion. The narrator explains that María Petronilla had only ever experienced submission to patriarchy and drew on that as her sole strategy of survival: "She had been too frightened to show resentment against [Santiago's] domination in the early days of their marriage and had protected herself with the armor of meek submission" (González and Eimer 1996, 85). Contra Doña Dolores, María Petronilla does not appear to have a matriarchal inheritance from which to draw strength. Her differential consciousness, therefore, works by remembering the future through a mystic form of time: prophesy. When Santiago sends Alvaro to join the guerrilla fighter, Antonio Canales, María Petronilla tells him, "Remember this: your blindness and your hatreds will put a curse on the house of Mendoza y Soría and bring it heartbreak" (141). Unlike Doña Dolores, who constantly reminds

Santiago of the past, María Petronilla reminds him of the future. Building on a millennium and a half of hermeneutics and epistemology, Catholicism is marked with residual temporalities that predate modernity, coloniality, and nationalism. While Santiago imagines his hierarchical relationship to God as an organizing principle, the narrator and women of the novel utilize Catholic forms of time, like prefiguration, redemption, ritual, typology, and teleology, to move differentially within the novel.

The narrator in particular draws on biblical typology to invoke a messianic future signified through the novel's infants. Tecla, wife of the Mendoza y Soría shepherd, gives birth to a son early in the novel. Red McLane delivers the baby when he is passing by and gives the shepherd family the gift of a gold coin. The baby's birth is, in many ways, the opening of the Mendoza y Soría hacienda to Anglo-Americans, because Tecla and José's jacal becomes a space in which Red can return unnoticed by the don. Unaware of the circumstances of this birth, Don Santiago mentions the baby to Gabriel del Lago: "'Tecla's first born is a bit of an occasion to the women,' he explained with a laugh. 'It is just another *peon* and of small consequence,'" but the narrator responds, "And had there been someone to tell him that Destiny might use so lowly a thing as the birth of a *peon* to shape her ends, Don Santiago's laugh would have been long and loud. The birth of a *hidalgo*, yes, but never a *peon*" (González and Eimer 1996, 191). As with the sexual license Santiago gives Alvaro, this is one of a number of instances when the narrator elevates peons through the tradition of biblical inversion, where the last shall be first.

The messianic form of time projects a future of redemption accessible to and through peon children. The possibilities for Tecla's baby, or for Paz's grandson, Manuelito, lie outside the narrative. Their form of time recalls the closing statement of Jovita González's master's thesis concerning young, U.S.-educated Texas Mexicans: "Ahead of them lies a struggle of which they are to be the champions" (2006, 116). Even the thesis cannot imagine what lies beyond the struggle, only that Tejanas/os will be the champions of a deferred justice. The fact that this sentiment of future promise for the Tejana/o youth appears in a novel set in 1848 and in González's history thesis describing the 1927 present signals its messianic vision, a form of time outside the flow of modernity.

Lloyd Pratt describes messianic time in African American literature, and his analysis is relevant for Mexican American authors as well: "Slaveholders and the racist state sought to deny African Americans access to the past and the future, making them 'creatures of the present.' Yet this literature conceives of an experience of time precipitated by revolutionary action, that has the potential to reconnect African Americans to their ancestors and descendants in diaspora—not through an imagined experience of simultaneity but rather through a much more significant moment of shared justice" (2010, 185). Sandoval provides a similar description for Derridian *différance*, which shapes messianic time, calling it "'the interval that puts off until later the possible that is presently impossible'; it is the 'other' deferred" (2000, 148). And, to repeat Emma Pérez, "That which may not yet be—but will be—is the scenario created to satisfy desire" (1999, 109). I bring these three ideas together and include Sandoval's quote rather than Derrida's original because the dialogic hermeneutics are important. *Différance* becomes the "differential" in differential consciousness. Justice—as a desire of and for the radical other—is messianic in *Caballero* because not only has it yet to occur but it has yet to be imagined. Like the African American writers Pratt describes, messianic time connects Mexican Americans across periodization—1846, 1936, 1996—each waiting for a shared justice. As a reversal of the future anterior, messianic time is not "what will have happened" but Pérez's "that which may not yet be—but will be."

González and Eimer's messianic deferred justice may not be the radical openness to the "other" that Derrida (1996) and Sandoval (2000) describe— after all, like Ruiz de Burton, Otero, and De Zavala, Jovita González and Margaret Eimer's vision is marked by class and race prejudice—but it presents dialogic openness, awaiting the next voice and the desire not yet intelligible within historical circumscription. The characters on the margins of the narrative reveal the limits of desire and dialogue in *Caballero*. Bebout writes of Luis Gonzaga and Devlin's queer romance that these characters "leave the narrative geography [because] as their potential desires may be actualized, they must move beyond the imagination"; their "same-sex desire is literally unthinkable" (2015, 363). Peons' entrance into equitable economic relationships with Anglos is also unimaginable in the racialized time of U.S. modernity. Margins are precisely where differential consciousness and its iteration as third-time/space feminism exist—always between more than one ideological formation. *Caballero* examines the limits of narrative possibility when Susanita writes home after her marriage to Warrener. The narration of her writing is punctuated three times by what she cannot write:

> She could not tell them at home that the house was small with a hastily tacked on room for Paz.... "We are very comfortable in a nice house, and we are happy."... She put down the pen and looked at the hills again. It would not do to add that several of the *rancheros* were in town and the Señora de Olivares had looked right through her.... "Inez's *papa* and *mamá* forgave her and are in town now, and they are all going to the *rancho* for a while."... It was better to say no more, *papá* would not like to hear that they were all very happy and had been very nice to the Warreners too. (González and Eimer 1996, 291)

Susanita's narrative account is strategic, and so is *Caballero*'s, pushing the limits of what can be spoken but not crossing them, inserting partial messages to those who might understand. In this light Don Santiago is not the only one who failed to realize that an infant peon might herald a radical future of peace and justice. Differential temporal movement allows Mexican Americans to be not outside of U.S. modernity but always moving between modernity and something else, some other ideological formation of time in a decolonial moment of situated agency. To draw on López (2011) again, *Caballero*, like *The Squatter and the Don*, is a resistant narrative more than a narrative of resistance. It resists the closure of unified analysis and gestures toward an open future.

Afterword

The Discontinuous Inheritance of
Mexican American Literature

The four authors I have just discussed, along with numerous other nineteenth- and early twentieth-century Mexican American writers, are a part of Chicana/o literature's discontinuous past. Their loss to American literary history is a result of the *mean time*, which dispossessed Mexican Americans of not only land but also presence within U.S. modernity, simultaneously erasing Mexican Americans from U.S. history and disavowing their participation in economic and political processes. Early Mexican American writing demonstrates a facility with time that reads the United States' contradictory temporal formations against one another to highlight the U. S. colonization of time. In both its presence and its absence, early Mexican American writing troubles U.S. modernity. The literary inheritance that these Mexican American texts bring to Chicana/o studies is one of discontinuity and erasure—an inheritance that, ironically, manifested itself in Chicana/o literature's own differential time consciousness even before the inception of the recovery project.

Perhaps the most radical Mexican American restructuring of the past was the Chicano Movement's concept of Aztlán. José Aranda calls Aztlán the "organizing symbol for Chicano literature, especially in the 1970s" (2003, 62).

Based on the mythic homeland from whence the Mexica, or Aztecs, migrated to Tenochtitlán (the seat of their empire, where Mexico City now stands) and conceptualized by Chicano nationalists as the present-day U.S. Southwest, Aztlán is usually figured through spatial metaphors. But the Chicana/o refashioning of Aztlán was a bold historicotemporal move that worked to unite a constellation of social organizations and peoples, each with their own unique trajectories and forms of time. Rafael Pérez-Torres argues that Aztlán is an "empty signifier," ambiguous but imbued with "excessive meaning," because it signifies multiple and sometimes contradictory concepts (1997, 16). The Chicana/o myth of Aztlán is an example of what Roland Barthes theorizes in his semiotic analysis of modern myth as "speech of the oppressed" (2012, 148) and what, when deployed self-consciously, Chela Sandoval terms "meta-ideologizing" (2000, 111). That process takes a symbol or set of signs imbued with a particular history and ideology and fills them with new ideological meaning. By co-opting Aztec mythic origins through Aztlán, the Chicano Movement contested the U.S. myths of Manifest Destiny and Puritan origins.[1]

By rooting Chicana/o territorial claims in a pre-Columbian past, Aztlán displaced Anglo-American land rights by preempting the temporal logic of Anglo-American nativism, which had delegitimized Mexican American claims to belonging by depicting them as immigrants or foreigners (despite the fact that the U.S. Southwest was Mexican before it was part of the United States). At the same time Aztlán figures Chicana/o native belonging through ancestral migration and return. By claiming both rooted and migrant rights to the land of the U.S. Southwest, Aztlán signifies home for a Mexican American community whose *antipasados* are from both sides of the U.S.-Mexico border. Signifying a past that is mobile *and* fixed, Aztlán was an attempt to heal the colonial wound of 1848 and unify a community that had at times been divided between longtime residents and newer immigrants. "Three moments of contestation are evoked in the naming of Aztlán," Pérez-Torres explains: "the Spanish invasion of the Aztec Empire, the appropriation of Mexican lands by the United States in the nineteenth and twentieth centuries, and the immigration to (or reconquest of) the U.S. Southwest by Mexicanos and Central Americans in the contemporary era" (1997, 16). The transhistorical significance of Aztlán linked Chicanas/os across diverse groups beginning in the 1960s, including dispossessed rural descendants of Spanish-land grant-ees, urban Chicanas/os denied social services like adequate education and medical care, migrant farmworkers, and the growing number of Chicana/o intellectuals at U.S. universities. In addition to its multipronged historical referents, Aztlán unified diverse Chicanas/os through a utopic rhetoric of liberation and unity that promised future reclamation of the stolen homeland.

Despite its ability to bring together the many groups that composed the Chicano Movement, Aztlán's projection of utopic unification was also its undoing. Many scholars have since criticized an essentialist, cultural nationalist ethos that deployed the concept of Aztlán to delimit ethnic identity, enforce heteropatriarchal dominance, and appropriate indigeneity. These restrictive functions appear prominently in the Chicano nationalist manifesto, *El Plan Espiritual de Aztlán*, which was formulated at the Denver Youth Conference organized by Rodolfo "Corky" González in 1969 and widely circulated by attendees. *El Plan*'s preamble, from whence it takes its title, was written by the "poet laureate of Aztlán," Alurista (López 2008, 93). While the preamble has some of the essentialist markers of Chicano nationalism, such as its claim that "the call of our blood is our power," it is also ambiguous in its description of "the bronze people with a bronze culture" (Anaya, Lomelí, and Lamadrid 2017, 27–30). Marissa López argues that *El Plan* "actually puts forward experiential notions of Aztlán that argue for the national imaginary as a globalizing human force, a nuance that . . . is often lost on Alurista's detractors" (2011, 9). She goes on to analyze Alurista's unpublished poem, "History of Aztlán," which describes Aztlán as a unifying force for pre-Columbian peoples and contemporary Latin American nations alike. Indeed, the concept of Aztlán is capacious in its spatial and temporal imagery.

Through its basis in Aztec mythology, Aztlán and other popular Aztec iconography of the movement privileged Chicana/o indigenous heritage over Spanish heritage to counter Western colonialism's authorization of white-ness as the racial marker of modernity. In Corky González's iconic Chicano Movement poem "Yo soy Joaquín" (1967), the gringo, the *gachupin*, and the *gabacho* blur together as white colonizers to be expelled both physically and psychically from the Chicana/o community. By drawing on indigenous, pre-Columbian cosmology, Aztlán rejects not just Western colonization but also the modernity it brings. Aztlán's claim to indigeneity is dubious, however. As Aranda writes, "The Chicano/a Movement could never have succeeded in a contest with the American Indian Movement over native sovereignty as a political or moral right" (2003, 18). In this sense Aztlán functioned not so much to promote indigenous rights as to expose the irrationality of white nativist claims to sovereignty and dominance.

While Chicano nationalists would have been mortified by the comparison, there are many points of congruence between the rhetoric of Aztlán and the political rhetoric of Miguel Antonio Otero. Though one was rooted in working-class Brown identification and the other in whiteness and capitalism, both manipulate the temporal logic of continuity and progress. Otero refers to Nuevomexicanos as "native" in a move reminiscent of white nativists at the turn of the twentieth century, while *El Plan* focuses on the indigenous aspects of mestizo heritage to likewise claim native status in the U.S. Southwest. For both, nativism functions through a projection of organic belonging based on the continuous inhabitance of a particular space. At the same time *El Plan*'s preamble describes Chicanos as not just inhabitants but *"civilizers* of the northern land of Aztlán" (Anaya, Lomelí, and Lamadrid 2017, 27; italics added), much like Otero recast his own Nuevomexicano family as the civilizers and modernizers of New Mexico. It is significant that Chicano nationalism drew most heavily from Aztec iconography and cosmology rather than from other indigenous cultures. Spatially, Tenochtitlán links Chicana/o identity to New Spain and Mexico because Mexico City was the capital for these geographic formations as well as the Mexica people, but the choice to draw on Aztec iconography, specifically, also privileges the pre-Columbian civilization most noted for its own colonial empire—the Aztecs demanded tribute and military support from conquered territories almost one hundred years before the Spanish conquest of Tenochtitlán by Hernán Cortés.

Both Otero's and Chicano nationalism's rhetorics oscillate between historical positions as colonizer and colonized to claim sovereignty in the present. But, whereas Otero adapts the racialized logic of U.S. modernity and its privileging of whiteness and progress, Aztlán inverts the racialization of time, exposing the illogic of U.S. modernity through an equally illogical premodern epistemology. I do not call Aztlán illogical to denigrate the concept as less rational than Euro-American origin stories but to describe the way it disrupts modern colonial Euro-American logos. Lee Bebout explains, "Aztlán and other mythohistorical interventions do not simply contest metanarratives. Rather, because the mythohistorical orders individual and collective experiences, these interventions fundamentally challenge dominant ways of seeing the world" (2011, 14). By drawing on premodern cosmology for its own origin myth, the Chicano Movement brought modernity itself into question through a dialogic and hermeneutic engagement with premodern global history.

In addition to drawing on at least three temporal nodes of colonization in Chicana/o history (Spanish colonization, U.S. land appropriation, and U.S. persecution of Mexican immigrants), Aztlán also functions on three semiotic levels. First, on the most fundamental and direct semiotic level, Aztlán called for a separatist, sovereign nation carved from the territory that the United States took from Mexico in 1848. Second, "a more politically tenable, yet still radical vision of Aztlán," Bebout explains, "was to establish a territorial nation through community control. A nation within a nation, this nation called for Chicano control of businesses, schools, and other local institutions." This reformist, rather than revolutionary, vision of Aztlán produced the most lasting material effects in the form of Chicano studies programs and increased awareness of Latina/o political influence. The third level, which Bebout classifies as "less radical," is a metaphorical Aztlán that is the "spiritual homeland" (2011, 77). The spiritual version of Aztlán is the one produced by Chicana/o artists and intellectuals. Though less materially radical, the artistic deployment of Aztlán is the one that makes it flexible and responsive to the varying sociohistorical contexts of diverse Chicana/o communities. Aztlán's temporal responsiveness to the U.S. colonization of Mexican American time is most prevalent in the artistic rendition of a spiritual homeland.

El Plan describes Chicanas/os as a "people whose time has come" (Anaya, Lomelí, and Lamadrid 2017, 27), a stark contrast to the Treaty of Guadalupe Hidalgo's perpetually deferred "proper time (to be judged by the Congress of the United States)" for Mexican American inclusion (Griswold del Castillo 1990, 181). As a metaideological construction of Chicana/o temporal belonging, Aztlán's adaptability and multiplicity contrasts U.S. modernity's measured temporal austerity. "Although it evokes a Chicano homeland, Aztlán also foregrounds the construction of history within a Chicano context. The difficult articulation of Chicana/o history—a history that speaks of dispossession and migration, immigration and diplomacy, resistance and negotiation, compromise and irony—remains ever unresolved," Pérez-Torres writes (1997, 19–20). His description is akin to the dialogic temporality visible in early Mexican American writing. Aztlán stands in for erased, suppressed, and colonized Chicana/o history because it remains unresolved, like an unfinalizable dialogue of pasts, presents, and futures.

Aztlán is certainly not the only metaideologizing performed by twentieth-century Chicana/o writers and activists. Sandra Soto (2010, 66) and José Aranda (2003, 30) both envision the Chicano nationalist concept of Aztlán as a forerunner to the more complex and culturally responsive theorization of *mestizaje*, which is rooted in the Spanish Empire's historical classification of biracial, Spanish indigenous heritage but has come to signify the multiplicity inherent in Chicana/o identity. Chicana/o theorization of *mestizaje* developed in large part from Chicana feminists' reclamation of the cultural and historical figure Malintzin, or La Malinche, the indigenous translator and mistress of Hernán Cortés, traditionally depicted as *la vendida* or *la chingada* (the sellout or the fucked one) and the original mother of the mestizo race. Soto writes, "Just as the earlier appeal of Aztlán rested both on its ties to actual history and on the elusiveness and thus permeability of that history, the concept of the new mestiza takes its force both from the historical reality of *mestizaje* (the miscegenation of indigenous and Spanish peoples during—and as a part of—the conquest of Mexico) and from the cultural and ethnic fluidity that it evokes. . . . In the process of recuperating La Malinche and deconstructing her legacy of passive treachery, Chicana feminists have refashioned the meaning of *mestizaje*" (2010, 66). By reimagining Malintzin as an intelligent, culturally adept, multilingual woman who rose through many layers of persecution from the position of a slave to one of the most powerful women in New Spain, Chicana feminists like Alicia Gaspar de Alba, Pat Mora, Carmen Tafolla, and many others have made the mother of *mestizaje* an icon of adaptability and survival.

Indeed, Gloria Anzaldúa's *Borderlands/La Frontera* (1987), the urtext of postmovement Chicana/o theory, demonstrates the interrelation and succession of Aztlán by *mestizaje* through its own revision of La Malinche. The book opens with "The Homeland, Aztlán"—an account of the South Texas border and the hemispheric migration of its inhabitants' ancestors, spanning the past thirty-five thousand years—followed by Anzaldúa's reclamation of not only La Malinche but also the folktale specter La Llorona and the Aztec goddess Coatlicue. *Borderlands/La Frontera* displays Chicanas/os' discontinuous inheritance in both its content and form. While creatively reimagining figures of the past, it bends genre expectations almost to a breaking point. History, autobiography, philosophy, ethnography, journalism, epic, prose, and poetry all converge in the monograph to create a dizzying collision of chronotopes that enact, as much as they depict, the multiplicity and discontinuity of borderland epistemology.

While not all Chicana/o literature from the 1970s and 1980s participates in the metaideological work of rewriting historical symbols, this period of literary production tends heavily toward formal experimentation and an interest in the past, particularly through the period's preponderance of coming-of-age narratives; multiperspectival, communal accounts; and narrative use of memory to examine or reopen the past. Ramón Saldívar acknowledges the centrality of historical representation in his 1990 assessment of the Chicana/o literary canon, writing, "For Chicano narrative, *history* is the subtext that we must recover because history is itself the subject of its discourse. History cannot be conceived as the mere 'background' or 'context' for this literature; rather, history turns out to be the decisive determinant of the form and content of the literature" (5). The U.S. temporal colonization of Mexican Americans had done more than conceal a past that merely needed to be revealed through diligent archival work. Chicana/o literary studies, which had been institutionalized along with other Chicana/o studies programs as a result of pressure from students and community members during the Chicano Movement, developed its own historical paradigm to fill the discontinuous, spectral absence of Mexican American literary history in the United States. As with the movement's construction of an indigenous past through Aztlán, Chicana/o literary studies looked for an origin to anchor the field. Before the Recovering the U.S. Hispanic Literary Heritage project began (re)printing texts in the 1990s, the extensive nineteenth- and early twentieth-century Latina/o literary production in the United States was unknown to most scholars. Scholars, instead, looked to the folkloric tradition of *corridos*, or border ballads, for Chicana/o literary origins.

Raymond A. Paredes (1978), Ramón Saldívar (1990), José E. Limón (1994), and other early critics attributed the root of Chicana/o literature to Mexican Americans' working-class oral folk tradition, particularly corridos that recounted border heroes' defiance against Anglo domination. But the corrido became Chicana/o literature's origin at the moment of its decline as an organic oral tradition along the border. Américo Paredes, the patriarch of Chicana/o literature (already there is another "origin" in Don Américo himself), documented the corrido tradition in South Texas in one of the earliest works of (proto)Chicano scholarship, his 1958 folklore study of the ballad of Gregorio Cortez, *With His Pistol in His Hand* (2010). In contrast, Américo Paredes's fictional writing was marked by the absence or the disappearance of the corrido tradition—as if the inscription of the corrido as Chicana/o literature's origin also marks its absence from Chicana/o culture in the present (Saldívar 1990, 49; Sorensen 2008, 113). Unlike the ballad of Gregorio Cortez, literature from the movement through the 1990s rarely features a cohesive, subject-in-resistance as protagonist. Saldívar acknowledges that Chicana/o literature does not necessarily follow the corrido pattern: "Against such an essentialist and ahistoric view, I show how the *corrido* has served as much to incite narratives differing from its ideological base as it has informed narratives conforming to its world view" (1990, 48). Nonetheless, the corrido remains a foundational paradigm for the contestatory "dialectics of difference" (1990) that Saldívar charts across the literary history of Chicana/o narrative.

With a few notable exceptions, Chicana/o literary history from the 1950s to the 1990s looked to an imagined heritage that I call corrido-as-origin, much like Chicano nationalism looked to Aztlán for its origin story.[2] Like Aztlán, the corrido-as-origin paradigm is marked by historical absence that appears in the nostalgic recreation of a lost border-hero tradition or the supposed dialectic progression to a new form, in which the corrido persists as a residual trace. Though fixed by masculinist and contestatory content, the corrido-as-origin paradigm also presents a folk past that is fluid because of its imagined orality (the orality is imagined in the sense that literary scholars were often referencing Américo Paredes's written accounts of corridos). What Saldívar

(1990) gestures toward—and what Jesse Alemán (1998) later proves—is that the corrido is always-already dialogic.[3] Even in attempts to establish it as a foundation for Chicana/o literary aesthetics, the corrido-as-origin belies Chicana/o writing's discontinuous literary inheritance. Chicana/o literature of the 1970s and 1980s reflects the corrido's formal disunity more than its semantic resistance. As Alemán writes, "Despite authorial intention as well as the intentions of Chicano critics, a level of socio-discursive resistance always already inscribes Chicano literary production. These 'counter discourses' not only contest dominant constructions of class, gender, and ethnicity, but because Chicano discourse, as with Chicano culture, is dialogic through and through, it also challenges monologic constructions of Chicano identity and literature, inscribing instead, on a stylistic level, a socio-literary resistance to any unified world view" (1998, 58–59). Alemán extends Chicana/o literature's intrinsic dialogism to poetry as well as fiction, and the same could be said of Chicana/o theater. Canonical and noncanonical texts alike present dialogic exchanges that draw on various dialects of Spanish, English, and indigenous languages and their multiple oral and written traditions and thus, consciously or unconsciously, bring together multiple forms of time.

Perhaps the most canonical work of Chicana/o fiction to come out of the movement era is Tomás Rivera's *Y no se lo tragó la tierra*, which in both form and content expresses the loss and recuperation of time. Though the book references a lost year and contains twelve vignettes framed by the opening and closing reflections of an unnamed boy, there are few temporal markers to orient the reader through narrative progression. The vignettes present markedly different chronotopes: a mother's pleading prayer to exchange her life for that of her enlisted son; the protagonist's haunting memory of a murdered "wetback"; the disorienting and immobilizing anxiety of an agoraphobic woman; the loss and re-creation of a family's only picture of the son who died fighting in Korea; the perpetual motion of migrants traveling on a truck, musing about "cuando lleguemos [when we arrive]"; and numerous others.[4] There is no sequential unfolding or clear correspondence between the twelve vignettes and the twelve months of a year. Many of the narratives puncture time, often through trauma but also by questioning the repressive epistemology of Catholicism, as in the titular chapter, when the unnamed protagonist finds peace after cursing God.

The book ends with the protagonist under a house hoping to recover his lost year, wishing for wholeness that is not available in either linear narrative or personal memory. He decides to continue going under the house so that, in solitude, he can bring all of his memories together, but then "volvió a la situación del presente [he became aware of the present]." As he exits the crawlspace, the woman who lives in the house reflects on the boy's tragic family, thinking he has gone mad, that "está perdiendo los años [he is losing years]," but as he goes home "se dio cuenta de que en realidad no había perdido nada [he realizes that in reality he had lost nothing]." The boy finds solace, instead, in the hermeneutic reordering of his past: "Encontrar y reencontrar y juntar. Relacionar esto con esto, eso con aquello, todo con todo. Eso era. Eso era todo. [To discover and rediscover and piece things together. This to this, that to that, all to all. That was it. That was everything]" (1987, 75). In this sense the book is an extended foray into the dyshesion of Chicana/o temporal experience and the realization that it does not, in fact, signify loss but instead opens the possibility to discover and reorganize time on one's own terms.

Chicana/o works from this period draw on Spanish and English literary traditions, indicating that the dialogic "interlingual" characteristic Alemán (1998, 60) identifies in Chicana/o literature brings with it a complex interplay of temporally inflected genres and canons. For example, Ana Castillo's non-sequential novel *The Mixquiahuala Letters* (1986) was heavily influenced by Argentine writer Julio Cortázar's novel *Rayuela*, which also features rearrangeable chapters, and Ron Arias explains that his novel *The Road to Tamazunchale* was influenced by Gabriel García Márquez as well as the Spanish "cronistas of the exploration centuries," not to mention *Don Quixote*, whom the protagonist imitates throughout the novel (1987, 11). Linguistic multiplicity functions on the level of heteroglosia, where different dialects of the same language comingle, and on the dialogic level, where texts and genres intersect and interact. While heteroglosia and dialogism structure all novels according to Mikhail Bakhtin (1981), Chicana/o literature demonstrates a preternatural interest in genres and dialects that expose the ideological formation of time. Chicana/o authors expose time as a social construct, present Chicana/o experience through discontinuity, and pose the possibility of reordering time through memory and conscious reflection.

As a case in point, Alejandro Morales authored five Chicano novels in Spanish and English in the period between 1970 and 1991 that feature fragmented narratives and a concern with historical representation. Four of them, *Caras viejas y vino nuevo* (1975), *Reto en el paraiso* (1983), *The Brick People* (1988), and *The Rag Doll Plagues* (1992), present multigenerational narratives that question the possibility of progress. All five, including *La verdad sin voz* (1979), incorporate aspects of historical fiction as well. *The Rag Doll Plagues*, for example, spans three hundred years and features three distinct timescapes: 1788 Mexico City, 1970s Los Angeles, and late twenty-first-century LAMEX, a futuristic urban corridor between Los Angeles and Mexico City. Colonialism is the metaphoric cause of the plagues that appear in each book, and each subsides just as rumors of revolution begin to circulate. But revolution brings repetition rather than progress, as the protagonist, Dr. Gregory (Gregorio) Revueltas appears in each of the novel's three books, despite the fact that he never reproduces within the narrative. Likewise, the futuristic new Aztlán figured in LAMEX's "Triple Alliance" alludes to twentieth-century NAFTA participants and the Aztec triple alliance of Tenochtitlán, Texcoco, and Tlacopan in a historical repetition that fails to bring the promise of progress. In this future setting mestizo blood appears to cure the new plague, but only through the reinscription of domestic work and slavery: "Many MCMs [Mexico City Mexicans] moved right in with the families and signed an agreement to offer their blood for sale" (1992, 194). Throughout the novel Dr. Revueltas is accompanied by two specters, Papá Damían and Gregorio, who silently guide and comfort him. For Revueltas Chicana/o inheritance is a self-referential spectral presence, a repetition rather than a lineage.

Chicana/o literature's unique relationship to time and history is not the isolated feature of a few works but is, instead, visible across most texts produced in the postmovement era and many more since then. The subsequent recovery of a vast body of nineteenth- and early twentieth-century Latina/o literature has prompted a reassessment of Mexican American, Chicana/o, and Latina/o literary history that has had to look backward and forward in time, as the canon expands in both directions. Jesse Alemán (2016) playfully calls this double vision the "Diachronics of Difference" as he reflects on Ramón Saldívar's (1990) *Chicano Narrative: The Dialectics of Difference*, twenty-six years after that foundational monograph's publication. It seems fitting that Chicana/o literary history should arrive late—after its "origin" had already been located in the corrido—because Mexican American narrative has never been linear.

In the Mean Time looks to the Treaty of Guadalupe Hidalgo as a moment of U.S. temporal colonization for Mexican Americans, an articulation of the temporal stasis that U.S. modernity produced and used to justify Mexican American disenfranchisement. Yet it would be counterproductive to assert that 1848 is the start of Mexican American temporal dislocation. One could argue, instead, that temporal dislocation is a function of European colonization of the Western Hemisphere, which created the modernity-coloniality epistemology, as Anibal Quijano (2000) and Walter Mignolo (2005) have articulated. Likewise, one could read both recovered and recently written Chicana/o narratives' disjointed temporality as a function of the poststructuralist, postmodern moment, during which early texts were first selected for recovery and canonical Chicana/o works were penned. But to fix a single origin for Chicana/o narrative form would be to betray the shape of Mexican American literature itself. The unsettling of linear history is a constitutive feature of Mexican American writing that spans across time. The task at hand is to develop new conversations between texts in an open-ended, interanimating dialogue, "to discover and rediscover and piece things together" (T. Rivera 1987, 152).

NOTES

1. A note on terminology: There are a number of terms to describe the subjects of *In the Mean Time*: Latina, Latino, Latina/o, Latinx, Chicana/o, Mexican American, Tejano, Californiana, Hispanic, and the variations of these words that are each inflected with a specific and complex history. Here I use the regionally specific term "Hispano," which is rooted in a history of New Mexican's identification with Spanish colonization over and above Mexican nationalism. It is also clearer to contemporary readers than the term Otero used to self-identify, "native," which he did not associate with Native Americans, whom he called "Indians." I use the anachronistic term "Mexican American" most frequently because it adequately describes the group of former Mexican citizens who became U.S. citizens after the Treaty of Guadalupe Hidalgo. Mexican Americans of the period were more likely to identify themselves by regionally specific terms such as "Tejano," which I also use when speaking about a regionally specific group. I use the term "Chicana/o" in the afterword to denote Mexican Americans after the Chicano Movement who identified with the political consciousness of the movement and the field of Chicana/o studies that grew from it. I reference Latina/o studies less frequently as the more recent and broader field of work that encompasses all U.S. residents with ancestry from areas in the Western Hemisphere colonized by Spain, of which Chicana/o studies and Mexican American studies are a part. Last, I prefer the ending a/o for gendered Spanish identity markers, though I recognize the many merits of the "x" ending and the "@" ending. Three of the four main authors I discuss were women, and I want to acknowledge and emphasize that gender identity in the book's terminology.

2. Senate Committee on Territories, *Omnibus Statehood Bill: Report*, Cong. Rec., S. Rep. 2206, 57th Cong., 1st Sess. (1902), at 184.

3. See Coronado (2013) for an account of northern Mexico's pre-U.S. modernity as it appears in print culture throughout Spanish and Mexican Tejas.

4. While California, New Mexico, Arizona, and Texas were all a part of Mexico before the U.S. invasion, some of these regions also had alternative national imaginings, as northern California and Texas both rebelled against Mexico in attempts to form separate nations.

5. There have been and continue to be temporalities that are not part of modernity. See, for example, Deloria (1992), Rifkin (2017), and Dinshaw (2012).

6. Daylight savings time was a controversial plan to save energy during World War I. It was repealed and then reestablished during World War II. In 1996 the U.S. hegemony of time extended to Mexico, when that nation began observing daylight savings time after NAFTA reshaped economic relations within North America. The change fragmented Mexico's temporality, as northern states wanted to match U.S. daylight savings time and southern states wanted to shorten daylight savings time. In 2001 Mexican president Vicente Fox split the nation's daylight savings time practice so that northern and southern Mexico made the switch at different times. An article in the *Economist* about NAFTA's disruption of Mexican time displays the ontological othering of Mexicans still present in U.S. representations of Mexican temporality. It reads, "Time has never been a precise concept in Mexico. To be punctual for an appointment is rare, and to be at a party at the stated hour is considered almost bad manners. Now a surreal row over daylight saving time is threatening to shatter this already fragile notion of time into several different, and competing, pieces" ("Change of Tiempo" 2001, 1).

7. In addition to Padilla's (1993) references to early Mexican American autobiographies as schizophrenic, a number of other scholars have used this term to describe Mexican Americans or their writing. For example, Pitt (1966) has an entire chapter on Californios' "Schizoid Heritage." More recently, Gaspar de Alba (1998) describes the cultural schizophrenia that Chicano artists navigate.

8. This is not to say that individual scholars were not working on recovering Mexican American–authored texts. Indeed, Genaro Padilla began work on *My History, Not Yours* (1993), which recovered a number of Mexican American autobiographies in 1985 and compiled and edited a collection of Fray Angélico Chávez's short stories in 1987. Sánchez and Pita (1992) were already working on recovering *The Squatter and the Don* before the recovery project's inception. They and other scholars working on individual projects of historical and literary recovery came together within Recovering the U.S. Hispanic Literary Heritage to make a collective impact on Chicana/o scholarship. At the same time the University of New Mexico Press began its Pasó por Aquí series, which focuses specifically on recovering New Mexican historical texts.

1. TEMPORAL COLONIZATION

1. For information about sporadic time zones in the United States, see Carey (1992) and Prerau (2005).

2. Dowd's time zones ignored geography and convention entirely by following an exact grid. The revision by William Frederick Allen allowed for divergence from the grid up to a hundred miles. The U.S. Congress did not officially adopt the railroad time system until 1918.

3. See Sánchez and Pita (1992). The novel is also almost always contextualized through the 1851 California Land Act, referenced repeatedly in the text. The law opened all Spanish and Mexican land grants in California to litigation and was the primary means of dispossessing landed Californios after California became a state.

4. I draw on Rosaldo's (1989) notion of imperialist nostalgia here and apply it to late nineteenth-century U.S. writings of the Southwest.

5. See also, for example, Alemán (2002), Goldman (1999), John González (2010), Jacobs (2001), and Luis-Brown (1997).

6. In another temporal linkage, Don Mariano dies at approximately the same time on the next evening, Christmas night, after he calls his family to him just at the clock strikes eleven.

7. The communications-based economy becomes even more prevalent with the use of the telephone, a device that does not exist in the time of the novel but that the narrator references in chapter 2, imagining a telephone wire connecting Don Mariano's house with William Darrell's Alameda house, where both men were discussing the Alamars' land.

8. While dependency theory developed in the wake of World War II, Grosfoguel finds a parallel in debates of the 1870s regarding free market versus protectionist economies in Latin America (2000, 350).

9. These letters were published in a pamphlet titled *How Congressmen Are Bribed, the Colton Letters: Declaration of Huntington That Congressmen Are for Sale*. The publication date and the printer are unknown, but it was published near the end of the nineteenth century, sometime after 1888. A full, digitized copy is available through the California Digital Library (Huntington and Colton 1895).

10. See, for example, Aranda (1998), John González (2004, 2010), and Alemán (2002).

11. The title of Aranda's 1998 groundbreaking article, "Contradictory Impulses: María Amparo Ruiz de Burton, Resistance Theory, and the Politics of Chicano/a Studies," seems most apt for describing the multiplicity of Ruiz de Burton's work here.

12. I would like to thank Jesse Alemán for pointing out this interesting error.

13. Notably, Goldman writes, "Ruiz de Burton appropriates the historical romance only to use it against itself" (1999, 79).

2. THE LAND OF POCO TIEMPO

1. Otero's use of the term "native" may also be a subtle response to U.S. nativism of the time, which promoted immigration restrictions that targeted Chinese and eastern

European immigrants but degraded all non-Anglo peoples through political cartoons and other propaganda. Otero's use of the term is both an ironic reversal and a sign of his complicity in many of the nation's racial hierarchies during his life.

2. Indeed, Otero's complete omission of any reference to segregated cars highlights his race and class privilege in this respect. I draw on English's (2013) discussion of railroad segregation here.

3. The Lincoln County War, which Otero described extensively in his biography of Billy the Kid, began in 1878 as a dispute between two sets of businessmen and the lawmen and outlaws allied with them. James Dolan and Lawrence Murphy operated a business in dry goods and cattle that essentially held a monopoly over the town of Lincoln, where they set high prices for local ranchers and held government contracts to provide beef and other goods to the U.S. military and the Bureau of Indian Affairs. They also profited from cattle rustling and land-claims manipulation. In 1876 English-born John Tunstall and his partner, Alexander McSween, opened a rival store. Violence broke out when McSween refused to surrender a disputed insurance settlement to the Murphy-Dolan group, and their hired guns shot John Tunstall. Many landowning Nuevomexicanos supported the Tunstall-McSween faction because Murphy-Dolan ran the town of Lincoln as if they owned it. Billy the Kid worked for Tunstall and is the most famous participant in the Lincoln County War. Samuel Axtell was governor at the time of the Lincoln County War and owed significant debt to Murphy and Dolan's business, and he removed the U.S. deputy marshal, who had been an ally of Tunstall-McSween's, leaving only Murphy-Dolan-controlled lawmen in Lincoln County. Otero and his family were not directly involved in the war but were economically and ideologically aligned with McSween's side. Thus, Otero's account of the Lincoln County War in *The Real Billy the Kid* is, like his autobiography, a critique of corruption under the territorial system.

4. As a child, Otero meets "Buffalo" Bill Cody in volume 1 of his autobiography and is not impressed by him. He compares him to Wild Bill Hickok, a man he does admire, writing, "Buffalo Bill, on the other hand, was rather selfish and wanted all the pomp and grandeur to himself. I would not call him a brave man; he was much too cautious. He was smart enough to arrange matters so he would always be in the clear. . . . As a scout and Indian fighter he had many superiors (1935, 32–33).

5. See Holtby for an account of Thomas Benton Catron's negative effect on New Mexico statehood as a delegate to Washington when his actions exposed New Mexico's corrupt political practices to the nation (2012, 11–34).

6. Cong. Globe, 57th Cong., 2nd Sess. (1902), at 188–96.

7. For Nuevomexicano accounts that discuss the trauma of Kearney's invasion, see Chacón (1986) and Padilla's (1993) sections on Chacón and Juan Bautista Vigil y Alaríd, the Mexican governor of New Mexico at the time of Kearney's takeover.

8. Beveridge's justification for denying New Mexico statehood rested on the socio-logical hierarchy of racial development that he ascribed to, but he had political reasons as well. The Republican Party had dominated the national political scene since the 1896 election of William McKinley, which followed the 1894 election of a Republican majority for both the House and Senate. Beveridge, Roosevelt, and other Republicans feared that admitting too many western states would sway the balance of power in favor of Democrats. Nonetheless, some Republicans sided with statehood. For example, Otero found a strong ally in Matthew Quay of Pennsylvania by aiding the Pennsylvania Development Company's myriad enterprises in New Mexico (see Holtby 2012, 109–10).

9. Cong. Globe, 57th Cong., 2nd Sess. (1902), at 188–96.

3. SPECTERS OF RECOVERY

1. Adina writes her last name as "De Zavala," probably following the convention of her father, Augustine, who also capitalized the *D*. Her grandfather, Lorenzo de Zavala, used the traditional Spanish form. I follow the usage of each of these individuals when writing their names.

2. See, for example, Thobani (2018).

3. Other organizations have contributed to the publication of individual texts and are also listed, but the Rockefeller Foundation is the only one listed in every single publication.

4. Though De Zavala generated a great deal of publicity and forestalled the demolition for a while, the upper story of the long barracks was eventually demolished in 1913. She is still credited with saving the long barracks, perhaps because the first floor remains intact. For accounts of her battle for the Alamo, see Flores (1996) and Ables (1955). De Zavala's battle over the Alamo building was widely publicized during her life.

5. See Flores's (2002) discussion of the changing cityscape of San Antonio.

6. While De Zavala was twenty-nine years younger than Ruiz de Burton, she was forty-four years older than González and fifty-four years older than Paredes. This relation may be easy to forget because De Zavala was very active in historical recovery late into her life. She was also a member of the Texas Folklore Society during some of the same years as González.

7. Indeed, Tejana repression is pathologized by Flores in his comparative analysis with Jovita González: "Personal displacements such as this are not unheard of for Mexican women of this period. Writing about De Zavala's colleague and associate in the Texas Folklore Society, José Limón's comments concerning Jovita González are appropriate for De Zavala as well. She was, he says, 'unsupported by the luxury of a "growing ethnic-feminist consciousness," who perhaps only appears to "turn a blind eye" on her role as a historical writing subject with respect to her native

community." But in the case of De Zavala, it was not a lack of sight but a displaced sense of ethnic self that affected her" (1996, xlix). I would argue that ethnic feminist consciousness is not a luxury but a method of survival that De Zavala and González deployed in ways scholars have yet to fully unpack.

4. MODERNITY AND HISTORICAL DESIRE

1. See Limón (1994), introductions to González and Eimer (1996) and Jovita González (1997), Vizcaíno-Alemán (2017), and John González (2010), among others.
2. The chronological confusion that sets *Caballero* as a precursory text for *George Washington Gomez*, despite the fact that both were being written at the same time, is reminiscent of the error on the back of Ruiz de Burton's *Who Would Have Thought It?* that refers to *The Squatter and the Don* as that author's first novel. In both instances the chronology of literary recovery comes to replace the chronology of authorship.
3. In 1748 Bourbon reforms were just beginning to take hold in Mexico. For New Spain these reforms resulted in tightened Spanish control and sparked tremendous discontent from criollos, American-born peoples of Spanish descent, who were no longer allowed to hold upper-level government appointments and were replaced by officials from Spain. Don José Ramón appears to be criollo, as the foreword references a bell that his father, not Don José Ramón himself, had brought from Spain, and Susana Ulloa also appears to be criollo because, while she moves within the court of Mexico City, her father wants to remove her from "the desolate scions of nobility who were parasites of the court" (González and Eimer 1996, xxxviii). Yet it is unclear where José Ramón's political affinities lie. The "foreign doctrines" (xxxvi) and the perfidious influence that he seeks to escape in moving from Mexico City to the Texas frontier could be the French influence that came with Bourbon reforms, because the Bourbon monarchs maintained close ties with France and drew on French political structures for their own reforms. On the other hand, revolutionary text that purported Enlightenment ideas like republicanism and helped fuel criollo desires for freedom from Spanish oppression relied on a transatlantic system of ideas that "circulated to and from Europe, Spanish American, and the United States, from Paris, London, and Spain to New Grenada, and from there to Philadelphia, Washington DC, Mexico, Louisiana, and Texas (Coronado 2013, 18). Though this foreign influence of circulating texts postdates Don José Ramón's exodus from Mexico City, their ideals of revolution and self-governance seem more in line with the ideology that his character rejects. Either way both the Bourbon reforms and the later (resultant) circulation of revolutionary texts are iterations of modernity.
4. It is worth noting that Eimer "steadfastly refused to marry" (Cotera 2008, 207), and Jovita González, in her master's thesis, outlined the nineteenth-century Tejano system of arranged marriage (2006, 81, 119n11).

5. Pérez is here writing about the late twentieth-century pop star Selina. Though enacted in very different ways and in different times, there is nonetheless a parallel in the third-space feminist acts of these two Tejanas amid constricting patriarchal circumstances.

AFTERWORD

1. See Aranda (2003) for a detailed analysis of the Chicano Movement's refashioning of the U.S. Puritan origin myth.

2. Notable exceptions are Bruce-Novoa (1990), who theorized Chicano art, including literature, as the ordering of discontinuity and the perpetual creation and recreation of an "axis mundi." In a very different way, Padilla (1993), Rebolledo (1995), Kanellos (1993), and a handful of other scholars began envisioning different origins for Chicana/o literature because they had already begun examining nineteenth- and early twentieth-century Mexican American literature in the 1980s before the inception of the recovery project, which they helped found.

3. Saldívar references Bakhtin's (1981) concept of dialogism when he describes Chicano narratives' relation to the corrido but focuses more on narrative's dialogic inclusion of the corrido than the corrido form itself. While he also states that "the corrido does not in any homogeneous manner serve as the real or fictive 'origin' of Chicano narrative nor as a 'narrative paradise to be regained'" (1990, 47), that statement is belied by the title of his previous chapter, "The Folk Base of the Chicano Narrative." Alemán (1998) fully develops the idea that corridos are dialogic.

4. All translations of *Y no se lo tragó la tierra* are from the Arte Público bilingual edition, translated by Evangelina Vigil-Piñon.

REFERENCES

ARCHIVAL AND MANUSCRIPT MATERIALS

Anderson, Christopher. n.d. "De Zavala's Marker Lies in Basement." *San Antonio Express-News*, 1B–2B. Vertical File: Gen. Adina De Zavala Papers. Daughters of the Republic of Texas Library at the Alamo, San Antonio.

De Zavala, Adina. 1936. Letter to the editor. Newspaper clipping. Vertical File: Gen. Adina De Zavala Papers. Daughters of the Republic of Texas Library at the Alamo, San Antonio.

———. 1943. Untitled speech. Typescript. Box 2M 168. Adina De Zavala Papers. Dolph Briscoe Center for American History, University of Texas at Austin.

———. n.d.a. Daughters of the Republic of Texas to Dear Friend. Box 2M 190. Adina De Zavala Papers. Dolph Briscoe Center for American History, University of Texas at Austin.

———. n.d.b. "Purchase Fund Subscription List of the Ancient Government Palace." Box 2M 190. Adina De Zavala Papers. Dolph Briscoe Center for American History, University of Texas at Austin.

———. n.d.c. "Texas History: Written and Unwritten." Typescript. Box 2M 190. Adina De Zavala Papers. Dolph Briscoe Center for American History, University of Texas at Austin.

Driscoll, Clara. n.d. Letter to Proprietors and Managers of Texas Hotels. Box 2M 129. Adina De Zavala Papers. Dolph Briscoe Center for American History, University of Texas at Austin.

Huntington, Colis Porter, and David Douty Colton. 1895. *How Congressmen Are Bribed, the Colton Letters: Declaration of Huntington That Congressmen Are for Sale.* Library Digital Collections. University of California–San Diego. Last modified December 1, 2017. https://library.ucsd.edu/dc/object/bb8501047z.

Northwest Ordinance. 1787. National Archives Microfilm Publication M332. July 13. Roll 9. Miscellaneous Papers of the Continental Congress, 1774–1789. Record

Group 360. Records of the Continental and Confederation Congresses and the Constitutional Convention, 1774–1789. National Archives, Washington DC. www .ourdocuments.gov.

Otero, Miguel Antonio, II. 1904. Louisiana Purchase exposition speech. December 18. Typescript. MSS 21. Folder 13. Box 4. Miguel Antonio Otero Papers. Center for Southwest Research, University of New Mexico.

———. n.d. Letter to Citizens of New Mexico. Typescript. MSS 21. Folder 5. Box 4. Miguel Antonio Otero Papers. Center for Southwest Research, University of New Mexico.

Plessy v. Ferguson. 1896. Judgement. May 18. *Plessy v. Ferguson*, 163, 15248. Record Group 267. Records of the Supreme Court of the United States. National Archives, Washington DC. www.ourdocuments.gov.

Schmitt, Edmond J. P. 1901. *Copies from the Archives: A Collation of Kingsborough's Antiquities of Mexico*. San Antonio: Johnson Brothers. Box 2M 167. Adina De Zavala Papers. Dolph Briscoe Center for American History, University of Texas at Austin.

Texas Senate. 1955. Concurrent Resolution 51. April 27. *Senate Journal: 54th Legislature, Regular Session*, 896. Legislative Reference Library of Texas. lrl.texas.gov.

Treaty of Guadalupe Hidalgo. 1848. Exchange copy. February 2. Perfected Treaties, 1778–1945. Record Group 11. General Records of the United States Government, 1778–1992. National Archives, Washington DC. www.ourdocuments.gov.

PUBLISHED WORKS

Ables, L. Robert. 1955. "The Work of Adina De Zavala." Master's thesis, Centro de Estudios Universitarios, Mexico City College.

Alemán, Jesse. 1998. "Chicano Novelistic Discourse: Dialogizing the Corrido Critical Paradigm." *Multi-ethnic Literature of the United States* 23 (1): 49–64.

———. 2000. "Novelizing National Discourses: History, Romance, and Law in *The Squatter and the Don*." In *Recovering the U.S. Hispanic Literary Heritage*. Vol. 3, edited by María Herrera-Sobek and Virginia Sánchez Korrol, 38–49. Houston: Arte Público.

———. 2002. "Historical Amnesia and the Vanishing Mestiza: The Problem of Race in *The Squatter and the Don* and *Ramona*." *Aztlán: A Journal of Chicano Studies* 27 (1): 59–93.

———. 2006. "The Other Country: Mexico, the United States, and the Gothic History of Conquest." *American Literary History* 18 (3): 406–26.

———. 2016. "The Diachronics of Difference: Then, Now, and Before Chicanidad." In *Bridges, Borders, Breaks: History Narrative and Nation in Twenty-First-Century Chicana/o Literary Criticism*, edited by William Orchard and Yolanda Padilla, 25–39. Pittsburgh: University of Pittsburg Press.

Allen, Thomas M. 2008. *A Republic in Time: Temporality and Social Imagination in Nineteenth-Century America*. Chapel Hill: University of North Carolina Press.

Althusser, Louis. 1971. *Lenin and Philosophy and Other Essays*. Translated by Ben Brewster. London: New Left Books.

Anaya, Rudolfo, Francisco A. Lomelí, and Enrique R. Lamadrid. 2017. *Aztlán: Essays on the Chicano Homeland*. Rev. ed. Albuquerque: University of New Mexico Press.

Anderson, Benedict. 2006. *Imagined Communities: Reflections on the Origin and Spread of Nationalism*. New York: Verso. Originally published in 1983.

Anzaldúa, Gloria. 1987. *Borderlands/La Frontera: The New Mestiza*. San Francisco: Aunt Lute.

Aranda, José F., Jr. 1998. "Contradictory Impulses: María Amparo Ruiz de Burton, Resistance Theory, and the Politics of Chicano/a Studies." *American Literature* 70 (3): 551–79.

———. 2003. *When We Arrive: A New Literary History of Mexican America*. Tucson: University of Arizona Press.

———. 2016. "When Archives Collide: Recovering Modernity in Mexican American Literature." In *The Latino Nineteenth Century*, edited by Rodrigo Lazo and Jesse Alemán, 146–67. New York: New York University Press.

Aravamudan, Srinivas. 2001. "The Return of Anachronism." *Modern Language Quarterly* 62 (4): 331–52.

Arias, Ron. 1987. *The Road to Tamazunchale*. Tempe AZ: Bilingual.

Austin, Mary. 1932. "Why I Live in Santa Fe." *Golden Book Magazine* 16 (October): 306–7.

Ayala, Elaine. 2006. "Preservationist Adina De Zavala Getting Her Due as Historical Figure." *San Antonio Express News*, November 28, 1C, 3C.

Bakhtin, Mikhail Mikhailovich. 1981. *The Dialogic Imagination: Four Essays by M. M. Bakhtin*. Edited by Michael Holquist. Austin: University of Texas Press.

Barthes, Roland. 2012. *Mythologies*. Translated by Annette Lavers. New York: Hill and Wang.

Bebee, Rose Maris, and Robert M. Senkewicz, trans. and eds. 2006. *Testimonios: Early California through the Eyes of Women, 1815–1848*. Berkeley: Heyday Books.

Bebout, Lee. 2011. *Mythohistorical Interventions: The Chicano Movement and Its Legacies*. Minneapolis: University of Minnesota Press.

———. 2015. "The First Last Generation: Queer Temporality, Heteropatriarchy, and Cultural Reproduction in Jovita González and Eve Raleigh's *Caballero*." *Western American Literature* 49 (4): 351–74.

Beveridge, Albert. 1898. "March of the Flag." September 16. *Voices of Democracy: The U.S. Oratory Project*. University of Maryland. https://voicesofdemocracy.umd.edu/beveridge-march-of-the-flag-speech-text/.

Brady, Mary Pat. 2002. *Extinct Lands, Temporal Geographies: Chicana Literature and the Urgency of Space.* Durham NC: Duke University Press.

Bruce-Novoa, Juan. 1990. *RetroSpace: Collected Essays on Chicano Literature, Theory, and History.* Houston: Arte Público.

———. 2003. "Offshoring the American Dream." *CR: The New Centennial Review* 3 (1): 109–45.

———. 2005. "When West Was North: Spirits of the Frontier Experience, or Can the MacGuffin Speak?" *Kritikos: An International and Interdisciplinary Journal of Postmodern Cultural Sound, Text, and Image* 2 (December).

Burrington, Ingrid. 2018. "New Mexico's Sad Bet on Space Exploration." *Atlantic*, March 2.

Camarillo, Albert. 1984. *Chicanos in California: A History of Mexican Americans in California.* Golden State Series. Sparks NV: Materials for Today's Learning.

Carey, James W. 1992. *Communication as Culture: Essays on Media and Society.* New York: Routledge.

Carrigan, William D., and Clive Webb. 2003. "The Lynching of Persons of Mexican Origin or Descent in the United States, 1848 to 1928." *Journal of Social History* 37 (2): 411–38.

Castillo, Ana. 1986. *The Mixquiahuala Letters.* Tempe AZ: Bilingual.

Chacón, Rafael. 1986. *Legacy of Honor: The Life of Rafael Chacón, a Nineteenth-Century New Mexican.* Albuquerque: University of New Mexico Press.

"A Change of Tiempo in Mexico." 2001. *Economist*, North America ed., March 10. www.economist.com/the-americas/2001/03/08/a-change-of-tiempo-in-mexico.

Coronado, Raúl. 2013. *A World Not to Come: A History of Latino Writing and Print Culture.* Cambridge MA: Harvard University Press.

Cotera, María. 1996. "*Hombres Necios*: A Critical Epilogue." Afterword to González and Eimer 1996, 339–46.

———, ed. 2006. *Life along the Border: A Landmark Tejana Thesis.* College Station: Texas A&M University Press.

———. 2008. *Native Speakers: Ella Deloria, Zora Neale Hurston, Jovita González, and the Poetics of Culture.* Austin: University of Texas Press.

Cutler, John Alba. 2015. *The Ends of Assimilation: The Formation of Chicano Literature.* New York: Oxford University Press.

Davis, Colin. 2005. "Hauntology, Specters and Phantoms." *French Studies* 59 (3): 373–79.

Deloria, Vine. 1992. *God Is Red: A Native View of Religion.* 2nd ed. Golden CO: Fulcrum.

Derrida, Jacques. 1994. *Specters of Marx: The State of Debt, the Work of Mourning and the New International.* Translated by Peggy Kamuf. New York: Routledge.

———. 1996. *Archive Fever: A Freudian Impression.* Translated by Eric Prenowitz. Chicago: University of Chicago Press.

De Zavala, Adina. 1996. *History and Legends of the Alamo and Other Missions in and around San Antonio*. Edited by Richard Flores. 1917. Reprint, Houston: Arte Público.

Dinshaw, Carolyn. 2012. *How Soon Is Now: Medieval Texts, Amateur Readers, and the Queerness of Time*. Durham NC: Duke University Press.

Earlie, Paul. 2015. "Derrida's *Archive Fever*: From Debt to Inheritance." *Paragraph* 38 (3): 312–28.

English, Daylanne K. 2013. *Each Hour Redeem: Time and Justice in African American Literature*. Minneapolis: University of Minnesota Press.

Fabian, Johannes. 2002. *Time and the Other: How Anthropology Makes Its Object*. New York: Columbia University Press. Originally published in 1983.

Flores, Richard. 1996. Introduction to De Zavala 1996, v–lvii. Houston: Arte Público.

———. 1998. "Memory-Place, Meaning and the Alamo." *American Literary History* 10 (3): 428–45.

———. 2002. *Remembering the Alamo*. Austin: University of Texas Press.

Foucault, Michel. 1986. "Of Other Spaces: Utopias and Heterotopias." Translated by Jay Miskowiec. *Diacritics* 16 (1): 1–9.

Gaspar de Alba, Alicia. 1998. *Chicano Art inside/outside the Master's House: Cultural Politics and the CARA Exhibition*. Austin: University of Texas Press.

Goldman, Anne E. 1999. "'I Think Our Romance Is Spoiled,' or, Crossing Genres: California History in Helen Hunt Jackson's *Ramona* and María Amparo Ruiz de Burton's *The Squatter and the Don*." In *Over the Edge: Remapping the American West*, edited by Valerie J. Matsumoto and Blake Allmendinger, 65–84. Berkeley: University of California Press.

González, John Morán. 2004. "The Whiteness of the Blush: The Cultural Politics of Racial Formation in *The Squatter and the Don*." In Luz Montes and Goldman 2004, 153–68.

———. 2009. *Border Renaissance: The Texas Centennial and the Emergence of Mexican American Literature*. Austin: University of Texas Press.

———. 2010. *The Troubled Union: Expansionist Imperatives in Post-Reconstruction American Novels*. Columbus: Ohio State University Press.

González, Jovita. 1997. *Dew on the Thorn*. Edited by José Limón. Houston: Arte Público.

———. 2006. *Life along the Border: A Landmark Tejana Thesis*. Edited by María Eugenia Cotera. College Station: Texas A&M University Press.

González, Jovita, and Margaret Eimer (Eve Raleigh). 1996. *Caballero: A Historical Novel*. Edited by José Limón and María Cotera. College Station: Texas A&M University Press.

González, Rodolfo. 1967. "I Am Joaquín/Yo soy Joaquín." N.p.: privately printed by *El Gallo*.

Gordon, Avery F. 2008. *Ghostly Matters: Haunting and the Sociological Imagination.* Minneapolis: University of Minnesota Press.

Gould, Lewis L. 2001. *America in the Progressive Era, 1890–1914.* Seminar Studies in History. New York: Longman.

Griswold del Castillo, Richard. 1990. *The Treaty of Guadalupe Hidalgo: A Legacy of Conflict.* Norman: University of Oklahoma Press.

Grosfoguel, Ramón. 2000. "Developmentalism, Modernity, and Dependency Theory in Latin America." *Nepantla: Views from South* 1:347–74.

Gruesz, Kirsten Silva. 2002. *Ambassadors of Culture: The Transamerican Origins of Latino Writing.* Translation/Transnation. Princeton NJ: Princeton University Press.

———. 2012. "What Was Latino Literature?" *PMLA* 127 (2): 335–41.

Holtby, David V. 2012. *Forty-Seventh Star: New Mexico's Struggle for Statehood.* Norman: University of Oklahoma Press.

Horn, Calvin. 1963. *New Mexico's Troubled Years.* Albuquerque: Horn and Wallace.

Jackson, Helen Hunt. 1884. *Ramona.* Boston: Little, Brown.

Jacobs, Margaret D. 2001. "Mixed-Bloods, Mestizas, and Pintos: Race, Gender, and Claims to Whiteness in Helen Hunt Jackson's *Ramona* and María Amparo Ruiz de Burton's *Who Would Have Thought It?*" *Western American Literature* 36 (3): 212–31.

Jameson, Fredric. 1991. *Postmodernism, or The Cultural Logic of Late Capitalism.* Durham NC: Duke University Press.

———. 1999. "Marx's Purloined Letter." In *Ghostly Demarcations*, edited by Michael Sprinkner, 26–67. New York: Verso.

Johannessen, Lene M. 2008. *Threshold Time: Passage of Crisis in Chicano Literature.* Amsterdam, Netherlands: Rodopi.

Kanellos, Nicolás. 1993. Foreword to *Recovering the U.S. Hispanic Literary Heritage.* Vol. 1, edited by Ramón A. Gutiérrez and Genaro M. Padilla, 13–15. Houston: Arte Público.

———. 2012. "Recovering the U.S. Hispanic Literary Heritage." *PMLA* 127 (2): 371–74.

Kaup, Monika. 2005. "The Unsustainable *Hacienda*: The Rhetoric of Progress in Jovita González and Eve Raleigh's *Caballero.*" *Modern Fiction Studies* 51 (3): 561–91.

Larson, Robert W. 1968. *New Mexico's Quest for Statehood, 1846–1912.* Albuquerque: University of New Mexico Press.

Lazo, Rodrigo. 2010. "Migrant Archives: Routes in and out of American Studies." In *Teaching and Studying the Americas: Cultural Influences from Colonialism to the Present*, edited by Anthony B. Pinn, Caroline F. Levander, and Michael O. Emerson, 199–218. New York: Palgrave Macmillan.

Limón, José E. 1994. *Dancing with the Devil: Society and Cultural Poetics in Mexican-American South Texas.* Madison: University of Wisconsin Press.

———, ed. 1996. Introduction to González and Eimer 1996, xii–xxvii.

———. 1999. "Mexicans, Foundational Fictions, and the United States: *Caballero*, a Late Border Romance." In *The Places of History: Regionalism Revisited in Latin America*, edited by Doris Sommer, 236–42. Durham NC: Duke University Press.

López, Marissa. 2007. "The Political Economy of Early Chicano Historiography: The Case of Hubert H. Bancroft and Mariano G. Vallejo." *American Literary History* 19 (4): 874–904.

———. 2008. "The Language of Resistance: Alurista's Global Poetics." *Multi-ethnic Literature of the United States* 33 (1): 93–115.

———. 2011. *Chicano Nations: The Hemispheric Origins of Mexican American Literature*. New York: New York University Press.

———. 2019. "The Difference Latinidad Makes." *American Literary History* 31 (1): 104–21.

Luis-Brown, David. 1997. "'White Slaves' and the 'Arrogant Mestiza': Reconfiguring Whiteness in *The Squatter and the Don* and *Ramona*." *American Literature* 69 (4): 813–39.

Lummis, Charles. 1913. *The Land of Poco Tiempo*. New York: Scribner's Sons.

Martín-Rodríguez, Manuel M. 2003. *Life in Search of Readers: Reading (in) Chicano/a Literature*. Albuquerque: University of New Mexico Press.

Mignolo, Walter D. 2005. *The Idea of Latin America*. Blackwell Manifestos. Malden MA: Blackwell.

Montejano, David. 1987. *Anglos and Mexicans in the Making of Texas History, 1836–1986*. Austin: University of Texas Press.

Morales, Alejandro. 1975. *Caras viejas y vino nuevo*. Mexico City: Moritz.

———. 1979. *La verdad sin voz*. Mexico City: Moritz.

———. 1983. *Reto en el paraiso*. Ypsilanti MI: Bilingual.

———. 1988. *The Brick People*. Houston: Arte Público.

———. 1992. *The Rag Doll Plagues*. Houston: Arte Público.

Morson, Gary Saul, and Caryl Emerson. 1990. *Mikhail Bakhtin: Creation of a Prosaics*. Palo Alto CA: Stanford University Press.

Nieto-Phillips, John M. 2004. *The Language of Blood: The Making of Spanish-American Identity in New Mexico, 1880s–1930s*. Albuquerque: University of New Mexico Press.

Nora, Pierre. 1989. "Between Memory and History: Les Lieux de Mémoire." *Representation* 26:7–24.

Osborne, Peter. 1996. *The Politics of Time: Modernity and the Avant-Garde*. New York: Verso.

O'Sullivan, John. 1839. "The Great Nation of Futurity." *United States Democratic Review* 6 (23): 426–30.

———. 1845. "Annexation." *United States Democratic Review* 17 (85): 5–10.

Otero, Miguel Antonio, II. 1901. *Report of the Governor of New Mexico to the Secretary of the Interior*. Washington DC: Government Printing Office.

———. 1902. *Report of the Governor of New Mexico to the Secretary of the Interior.* Washington DC: Government Printing Office.

———. 1935. *My Life on the Frontier, 1864–1882: Incidents and Characters of the Period When Kansas, Colorado, and New Mexico Were Passing through the Last of Their Wild and Romantic Years.* Vol. 1. New York: Press of the Pioneers.

———. 1936 (1998). *The Real Billy the Kid: With New Light on the Lincoln County War.* Edited by John-Michael Rivera. Houston: Arte Público.

———. 1939. *My Life on the Frontier, 1882–1897: Death Knell of a Territory and Birth of a State.* Vol. 2. Albuquerque: University of New Mexico Press.

———. 1940. *My Nine Years as Governor of the Territory of New Mexico, 1897–1906.* Albuquerque: University of New Mexico Press.

Padilla, Genaro M. 1993. *My History, Not Yours: The Formation of Mexican American Autobiography.* Madison: University of Wisconsin Press.

Paredes, Américo. 2010. *With His Pistol in His Hand: A Border Ballad and Its Hero.* Austin: University of Texas Press.

Paredes, Raymond A. 1978. "The Evolution of Chicano Literature." *MELUS* 5 (2): 71–110.

Pérez, Emma. 1999. *The Decolonial Imaginary: Writing Chicanas into History.* Bloomington: Indiana University Press.

Pérez, Vincent. 2000. "Teaching the Hacienda: Juan Rulfo and Mexican American Cultural Memory." *Western American Literature* 35 (1): 33–44.

———. 2004. "Remembering the Hacienda: History and Memory in Jovita González and Eve Raleigh's *Caballero: A Historical Novel.*" In *Look Away! The U.S. South in New World Studies,* edited by Jon Smith and Deborah Cohn, 471–94. Durham NC: Duke University Press.

Pérez-Torres, Rafael. 1997. "Refiguring Aztlán." *Aztlán: A Journal of Chicano Studies* 22 (2): 15–41.

Perkins, Maureen. 2001. *The Reform of Time: Magic and Modernity.* Sterling VA: Pluto.

Pitt, Leonard. 1966. "Schizoid Heritage." In *The Decline of the Californios,* 277–96. Berkeley: University of California Press.

Pratt, Lloyd. 2010. *Archives of American Time: Literature and Modernity in the Nineteenth Century.* Philadelphia: University of Pennsylvania Press.

Prerau, David. 2005. *Seize the Daylight: The Curious and Contentious Story of Daylight Saving Time.* New York: Thunder Mountain.

Quijano, Anibal. 2000. "Coloniality of Power, Eurocentrism, and Latin America." *Nepantla: Views from the South* 1 (3): 533–80.

Ramírez, Francisco P. 1855. Editorial. Translated by Pablo Peschiera. *El Clamor Público* (Los Angeles), July 24.

Rebolledo, Tey Diana. 1990. "Narrative Strategies of Resistance in Hispana Writing." *Journal of Narrative Technique* 20 (2): 134–46.

———. 1995. *Women Singing in the Snow: A Cultural Analysis of Chicana Literature*. Tucson: University of Arizona Press.

Rifkin, Mark. 2017. *Beyond Settler Time: Temporal Sovereignty and Indigenous Self-Determination*. Durham NC: Duke University Press.

Rivera, John-Michael, ed. 1998. Introduction to Otero 1998, xi–xliv.

———. 2000. "Miguel Antonio Otero II, Billy the Kid's Body, and the Fight for New Mexican Manhood." *Western American Literature* 35 (1): 46–57.

———, ed. 2005. Introduction to *Journey to the United States of North America/Viaje a los Estados Unidos del Norte de América*, by Lorenzo de Zavala, vii–xxxiii. Houston: Arte Público.

———. 2006. *The Emergence of Mexican America: Recovering Stories of Mexican Peoplehood in U.S. Culture*. New York: New York University Press.

———. 2007. "The Archive as Specter." *English Language Notes* 45 (1): 1–4.

Rivera, Tomas. 1987. . . . *Y no se lo tragó la tierra* / . . . *And the Earth Did Not Devour Him*. Translated by Evangelina Vigil-Piñon. Arte Público bilingual ed. Houston: Arte Público.

Rodríguez, J. Javier. 2008. "*Caballero*'s Global Continuum: Time and Place in South Texas." *Multi-ethnic Literature of the United States* 33 (1): 117–38.

Roosevelt, Theodore. 1906. "The President's Plea for Arizona's Assent." Special to the *New York Times*, July 4.

Rosaldo, Renato. 1989. "Imperialist Nostalgia." *Representations* 26 (Spring): 107–22.

———. 1993. *Culture and Truth: The Remaking of Social Analysis*. Boston: Beacon.

Ruiz de Burton, María Amparo. 1992. *The Squatter and the Don: A Novel Descriptive of Contemporary Occurrences in California*. Edited by Rosaura Sánchez and Beatrice Pita. 1885. Reprint, Houston: Arte Público.

———. 1995. *Who Would Have Thought It?* Edited by Rosaura Sánchez and Beatrice Pita. 1872. Reprint, Houston: Arte Público.

Rydell, Robert W. 1984. *All the World's a Fair: Visions of Empire at American International Expositions, 1876–1916*. Chicago: University of Chicago Press.

Saldívar, Ramón. 1990. *Chicano Narrative: The Dialectics of Difference*. Madison: University of Wisconsin Press.

Sánchez, Rosaura. 1995. *Telling Identities: The Californio Testimonios*. Minneapolis: University of Minnesota Press.

Sánchez, Rosaura, and Beatrice Pita. 1992. Introduction to Ruiz de Burton 1992, 7–50.

———, eds. 2001. *Conflicts of Interest: The Letters of María Amparo Ruiz de Burton*. Houston: Arte Público.

Sandoval, Chela. 2000. *Methodology of the Oppressed*. Minneapolis: University of Minnesota Press.

Seguín, Juan N. 2002. *A Revolution Remembered: The Memoirs and Selected Correspondence of Juan N. Seguín*. Edited by Jesus F. de la Teja. Fred H. and Ella Mae More Texas History Reprint Series. Austin: Texas State Historical Association Press.

Sewell, William H., Jr. 2008. "The Temporalities of Capitalism." *Socio-economic Review* 6:517–37.

Slotkin, Richard. 1973. *Regeneration through Violence: The Mythology of the American Frontier 1600–1860*. Norman: University of Oklahoma Press.

Sommer, Doris. 1991. *Foundational Fiction: The National Romances of Latin America*. Berkeley: University of California Press.

Sorensen, Leif. 2008. "The Anti-*corrido* of *George Washington Gómez*: A Narrative of Emergent Subject Formation." *American Literature* 80 (1): 111–40.

Soto, Sandra K. 2010. *Reading Chican@ Like a Queer: The De-mastery of Desire*. History, Culture, and Society Series, Center for Mexican American Studies. Austin: University of Texas Press.

Strom, Stephanie. 2004. "A.C.L.U. Rejects Foundation Grants over Terror Language." *New York Times*, October 19.

Tatum, Charles. 1993. "Canon Formation and Chicano Literature." In *Recovering the U.S. Hispanic Literary Heritage*. Vol. 1, edited by Ramón A. Gutiérrez and Genaro M. Padilla, 199–208. Houston: Arte Público.

Thobani, Sunera. 2018. "Multiculturalism and Western Exceptionalism: The Cultural Politics of the West." *Fudan* 11 (2): 161–74.

Torres, Héctor. 1986. "Discourse and Plot in Rolando Hinojosa's *The Valley*: Narrativity and the Recovery of Chicano Heritage." *Confluencia* 2 (1): 84–93.

Turner, Frederick Jackson. 1993. "The Significance of the Frontier in American History." In *History, Frontier, and Section: Three Essays by Frederick Jackson Turner*, edited by Martin Ridge, 59–91. Albuquerque: University of New Mexico Press.

Viego, Antonio. 2007. *Dead Subjects: Toward a Politics of Loss in Latino Studies*. Durham NC: Duke University Press.

Vigil, Maurilio E. 1980. *Los Patrones: A Profile of Hispanic Political Leaders in New Mexico History*. Washington DC: University Press of America.

Vizcaíno-Alemán, Melina. 2017. *Gender and Place in Chicana/o Literature: Critical Regionalism and the Mexican American Southwest*. New York: Palgrave.

INDEX

Buffalo Bill Cody, 58, 150n4

Caballero (González and Eimer), 18, 22–
23, 107, 109–20, 124–26, 130–33
California: anti–Mexican American laws
in, 3–5; history of land politics in, 3,
41–42, 148n4, 149n3; missions, 31–
32; statehood of, 3, 62, 149n3
California Land Act (1851), 3, 31, 41–42,
149n3
Californio community, 27–31, 44
Camarillo, Albert, 28
capitalism, 7; and dependency theory,
38–39, 44, 62, 149n8; and historical
recovery, 22, 80–82, 85–87, 91–93; tem-
poral manipulation through, 9, 36, 41;
and western expansion, 19–20, 27, 47
Carey, James W., 25, 37
Casis, Lilia, 106
Castillo, Ana, 144
Catholic missions, 31–32
Catron, Thomas Benton, 56, 67–68, 74,
150n5
Central Pacific Railroad, 28, 34, 39
Chicana feminism, 15, 107–9, 114. *See
also* feminism
Chicana/o, term of, 147n1
Chicana/o studies, discipline of, 147n1
Chicano Movement, 135–42, 147n1
Chicano Narrative (Saldívar), 145–46
Chicano Nations (López), 48
chronotope, 7, 26, 31–32, 113–14, 141, 143.
See also temporal colonization
citizenship, 2–3, 61–62, 64–65, 147n1
Civil Rights Act (1957), 1
Cleveland, Grover, 57–58
coloniality, 5, 146. *See also* modernity;
temporal colonization
Colton, David, 41

commodity fetishism, definition of, 90
communications-based economy, 37,
149n7
congressional bribery, 41, 149n9
Copies from the Archives (Schmitt), 100
Coronado, Raúl, 5, 116–17
Coronel de Agreda, Mary, 103–4
corridos, 23, 142–46, 153n3
Cortázar, Julio, 144
Cortez, Gregorio, 142
Cotera, María, 106, 112–13
criollos, 152n3
cultural schizophrenia, 14–15, 148n7
Cutler, John Alba, 129

Dancing with the Devil (Limón), 105,
106, 151n7
Daughters of the Republic of Texas
(DRT), 22, 79–80, 88–89, 93
Davis, Colin, 99
daylight savings time, 9, 148n6. *See also*
time zones
debt, definition of, 91, 96
de facto segregation, 3
dependency theory, 38–39, 44, 62, 149n8
Derrida, Jacques, 81, 95–96, 100, 123
De Zavala, Adina, 12; and the Alamo,
18, 21–22, 79–80, 87–94, 151n4;
heritage of, 97–99, 151n7; *History
and Legends of the Alamo*, 22, 79–85,
90, 103–4; "The Padre's Gift," 82–84,
96; political work of, 18; spelling of
name of, 151n1; and Texas Historical
Landmarks Association, 93–94; and
textual recovery, 16, 96–99
de Zavala, Lorenzo, 88, 98, 99, 151n1
De Zavala Daughters (chapter of DRT),
88, 93. *See also* Daughters of the
Republic of Texas (DRT)

dialogism, 19, 112–13, 142–46, 153n3
differential consciousness, 12, 14–15, 17, 47, 57, 112, 114, 115, 128, 130, 132–33
differential time consciousness, 9–15, 17, 18, 21, 47–48, 55, 109, 119, 130, 135. *See also* temporal colonization
Dobie, J. Frank, 105, 106, 120
Don Quixote de la Mancha (Cervantes), 144
Dowd, Charles, 25
Driscoll, Clara, 22, 88, 89–90, 92
DRT. *See* Daughters of the Republic of Texas (DRT)

Earlie, Paul, 91
economic value of recovery, 22, 80–82, 85–87, 91–93. *See also* capitalism
Eimer, Margaret. See *Caballero* (González and Eimer)
El Plan Espiritual de Aztlán, 137
English, Daylanne K., 11

Fabian, Johannes, 39, 70
feminism: Chicana, 15, 107–9, 114; and ethnic-feminist consciousness, 151n7; third-space, 115, 125, 132–33, 153n5
Flores, Richard, 85, 89, 91, 98, 119
Foucault, Michel, 91
Fox, Vicente, 148n6
free market vs. protectionist economy, 149n8. *See also* capitalism; economic value of recovery
Frontier Thesis, 9, 30, 50, 52. *See also* Manifest Destiny; Turner, Frederick Jackson
futurity, 8, 36–39, 77, 117. *See also* messianic time; temporal colonization

García Márquez, Gabriel, 144
Gaspar de Alba, Alicia, 14

gendered terminology, 147n1
Goldman, Anne, 46, 149n13
González, John Morán, 46, 118, 125–26
González, Jovita, 12; *Caballero*, 18, 22–23, 107, 109–20, 124–26, 130–33; José Limón's description of, 105, 151n7; *Life along the Border*, 107–8, 129–30, 131; political work of, 18, 106; on textual recovery, 16
González, Rodolfo "Corky," 137, 138
Gordon, Avery, 17, 101, 104
Gould, Lewis L., 60
Greaser Act. *See* Anti-Vagrancy Act (1855)
"The Great Nation of Futurity" (O'Sullivan), 8
Grenet, Honoré, 88
Griswold del Castillo, Richard, 62, 67
Gruesz, Kirsten Silva, 13, 16, 86

haciendados, 11, 124, 129
Harlan, John Marshall, 53
hauntological, definition of, 99
Hispano, term of, 147n1
historical commodity fetishism, definition of, 90
historical recovery: of the Alamo, 18, 21–22, 79–80, 151n4; temporal economy of, 80, 85–87, 91–93. *See also* textual recovery
History and Legends of the Alamo (De Zavala), 22, 79–85, 90, 103–4. *See also* De Zavala, Adina
"History of Aztlán" (Alurista), 137
Hugo and Schmeltzer Firm, 88
Huntington, Collis, 41

Imagined Communities (Anderson), 6–7
Immigration Restriction League, 60, 74

inheritance, 43, 45, 80, 96

IN THE POSTWESTERN HORIZONS SERIES

*Dirty Wars: Landscape, Power, and
Waste in Western American Literature*
John Beck

Post-Westerns: Cinema, Region, West
Neil Campbell

*The Rhizomatic West: Representing
the American West in a
Transnational, Global, Media Age*
Neil Campbell

Weird Westerns: Race, Gender, Genre
Edited by Kerry Fine, Michael
K. Johnson, Rebecca M. Lush,
and Sara L. Spurgeon

*Positive Pollutions and Cultural
Toxins: Waste and Contamination in
Contemporary U.S. Ethnic Literatures*
John Blair Gamber

Dirty Words in Deadwood:
Literature and the Postwestern
Edited by Melody Graulich
and Nicolas Witschi

*True West: Authenticity and
the American West*
Edited by William R. Handley
and Nathaniel Lewis

Teaching Western American Literature
Edited by Brady Harrison
and Randi Lynn Tanglen

*We Who Work the West: Class,
Labor, and Space in Western
American Literature*
Kiara Kharpertian
Edited by Carlo Rotella and
Christopher P. Wilson

*Captivating Westerns: The Middle
East in the American West*
Susan Kollin

*Postwestern Cultures:
Literature, Theory, Space*
Edited by Susan Kollin

Westerns: A Women's History
Victoria Lamont

CPSIA information can be obtained
at www.ICGtesting.com
Printed in the USA
LVHW111304090320
649414LV00005B/43